MOLD

is a Four-Letter Word

My Unintentional Journey

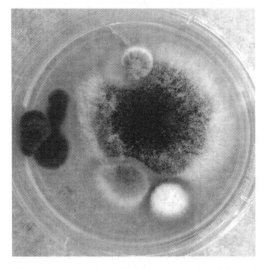

Under the category of "You can't make this stuff up", if you are into the health impacts and politics of mold, office politics, conspiracy theories and government inadequacies and corruption, this book is for YOU! It also has helpful information on understanding narcissists and sociopaths and the challenges of super tall people.

FRANCIS BRIGHTON

author HOUSE®

AuthorHouse™
1663 Liberty Drive
Bloomington, IN 47403
www.authorhouse.com
Phone: 833-262-8899

Published by AuthorHouse 09/27/2021

ISBN: 978-1-6655-3740-7 (sc)
ISBN: 978-1-6655-3739-1 (e)

Library of Congress Control Number: 2021918392

Print information available on the last page.

MY STORY

So there I was, home from work, lying in bed with blood in my urine, a kidney infection, nose bleeds, ear infections in both ears, a sinus infection and various other problems. To say I didn't feel well was an understatement. WTF? What has happened to me? Just a couple years ago I played in women's basketball and softball leagues. My basketball team won three league championships and my softball team won one. (The only thing I got for winning four championships was lousy t-shirts.) At 51 years old, I was the oldest player in my women's basketball league. My high game was a triple double with 29 points, 17 rebounds and 10 assists. OK, I does help that I'm 6'-3" tall and played intercollegiate basketball at Oklahoma State University but the league did include some good high school and college players trying to get playing time to improve their games.

So how did I go from league champion to deathly ill in such a short time? I was soon to discover the answer was a four letter word: MOLD. This story will explain my journey to discover the cause of my illness, the politics that prevents getting proper medical diagnosis and treatment, and what I did to detect the problems and overcome my illness and symptoms and recover from a deadly fungal infection called Aspergillosis.

In order for you to understand some of the facts of my illness, I need to tell you some background information. I was born in Chicago in 1958 with a cleft lip and palate to a very tall family. My dad and uncles on both sides of my family and their male cousins are all around 6'-4" tall or taller. My mother and grandmothers and aunts were between

5'-9" and 5'-11", very tall for women of that era. My sister and my two brothers are all around 6'-5".

A cleft lip and palate happens in utero when the two plates of the skull that form the hard palate do not completely fuse together. Around 1 in 700 children have a cleft lip and/or palate. No particular causes have been identified but it is considered to be caused by a combination of genetic and environmental factors. In 1958, babies with cleft palates usually had surgery at around 6 months of age when they have grown enough to tolerate surgery. Not surprisingly, I was a very large baby and I was able to have my first surgery at six weeks old. As a child I had a number of subsequent surgeries to the lip and palate as well as ear surgeries. The Eustachian tubes of a child with the cleft lip and palate are frequently different structurally and ear infections and corrective surgeries are common. I was always told that the doctors who had done my lip and palate surgeries had done a good job. I am eternally grateful to all of the doctors and nurses who performed my surgeries to help me have a fairly normal face and life.

When I was around 25, I still had the remnants of some surgical scars underneath my left nostril. I had always been told that there was a surgery called a Z-plasty that could be done to correct it and I felt that it was time to have the surgery. I also had two fistulas (openings from one area to another) where the surgeries never completely closed. One was a hole in the roof of my mouth that went up inside my left nasal passage and the other was a hole that went up above front of my teeth underneath my lip and gum up to the floor of my sinus. I could drink milk and force it up through either hole and make it come out my nose. Also, if I had a cold, the mucous would drain down from my nose into my mouth. I also did get an occasional sinus infection but this and the fistulas were of little concern to me, all I cared about was the cosmetic look of the small scar under my nostril. So I went to one of the surgeons in Los Angeles that specialized in cleft palate surgeries. My x-ray showed a gap in the bone where the fistulas were. All I wanted was a little revision to the scar.

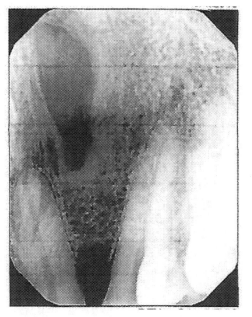

X-Ray showing a hole in the bone

I was previously told the scar could be fixed with a simple procedure but this surgeon's recommendation was a surgery he was specializing in to do a bone graft to fill in the gap in the bone that would prevent germs from traveling from my mouth to my nose and eliminate the sinus infections. To do the bone graft, they use a borrow site on the skull where they scraped bone from. They make a cut in the hair and shave the bone off the skull and pack it into the hole. I had the surgery and unfortunately, I had complications following the surgery. I had a continuous severe sinus infection I could not get rid of. The shards of bone that had been grafted in gradually worked their way out through the skin and tissues. One by one small shards of bone popped through the skin in the roof of my mouth, through the floor of my nose and through the gums above my front teeth leaving the tissue like a Swiss cheese of bone holes. I had pain and sinus infections. I went back to the doctor numerous times and he denied that there were any problems, but something was seriously wrong. I went to another ear, nose and throat specialist. He knew the doctor who had done the surgery. He would not acknowledge any problems but gave me a prescription for antibiotics and sent me on my way. The problems persisted and I was on antibiotics for six months straight.

As I went to other doctors, I realized they were reluctant to comment on any other Doctor's surgery and were not straight forward with me. I was determined to get to the bottom of this. I looked up all of the craniofacial teams, and doctors specializing in cleft palate or similar problems in the Los Angeles and surrounding areas. All in all I went to eleven different doctors and I got ten different answers ranging from there was nothing wrong to that I needed an array of other minor and major surgeries. I got the feeling from all the doctors there was a concern about being involved in a medical issue that could become part of a malpractice problem and they were reluctant to become involved. It took a lot of tenacity to make and go to all of these appointments and it was an emotional roller coaster trying to deal with and sort through the proposed solutions. It is really depressing to go to a specialist that you believe can help you only to be told they will not get involved or there is nothing they can do. Out of the eleven specialists I went to, I only got two answers that matched and that was the diagnosis I was going to go with. I will always be grateful to the Doctor, who worked at a low key government facility at the time, for nailing the diagnosis. The bone around the graft was infected. There was no way to heal from this unless they went back in surgically to scrape out the infection followed by extended anti-biotics. I was devastated to find out I needed to have surgery again.

Once I had the diagnosis, I sought out the proper team to do the surgery. I would not tell the doctors I went to who had done this surgery that had gone bad. Surely he was one of their colleagues or golfing buddies. The craniofacial world is pretty small. I met with the craniofacial team at a well known medical facility. The team consists of about eight different specialists. Each prospective patient meets with the team members. Then the team will have a meeting to discuss each of the patients and come up with a plan. They came up with two surgeons who were going to team up. One ear, nose and throat surgeon would correct some problems in my sinuses and the other would remove the bone infection and ultimately do reconstructive work that would close both of the fistulas. I love this hospital and I am grateful for these skillful surgeons.

At the present time, I still have a deviated septum, a hole in my septum, areas in my sinus where the two sides of the nasal passage have fused together, a hole in the bone where the bone graft used to be, a fistula, collapsed nasal valve and various other problems. The doctor's see me walk in the office and they all start thinking: "Ka-Ching $$$" and recommend whatever procedure is their specialty.

I also had an injury that resulted in a torn meniscus in my knee, torn sacro-iliac joint in my lower back and a torn rotator cuff in my shoulder. All in all to date I have had around sixteen surgeries and one of my goals in life has been to never have any surgery ever again. This goal is challenged every time I go to the doctor. I have yet to meet and Ear, Nose and Throat doctor that has not recommended a surgical procedure they could do. To date I have a list of around ten different procedures that have been proposed. In my teens I was advised that any surgeries I had in the future should be done by cleft palate or craniofacial specialists. I felt that many of the ENT's who proposed surgeries were entirely unqualified to deal with my problems. I have also been told by the doctors who did my last surgery that I should avoid any future sinus surgeries if at all possible due to the scarring from all the previous surgeries, the poor circulation and the limited blood supply to the tissues.

I worked for about 23 years at a couple different local government agencies. There was no shortage of scandals and stories. The first big shocking event was when my supervisor, a fairly high official at a local government office where I worked was arrested and taken out of the office in Handcuffs during work hours for accepting bribes in exchange for approving plans. The head official had refused to sign them as they included building new homes in a flood hazard area without mitigating the flood problem. The head official eventually quit. The political pressure to sign and approve the problematic plans was too much. He kept saying, I'd rather lose my job than my professional License. He moved to the California coast and had a nice life building and selling spec homes on the coastal hillsides.

Another notable incident was part of the swath of destruction left by a sociopathic manager. She was a very poor manager with inadequate management skills. First, she started sleeping with the Head Assistant Manager and no one would complain about her. She would target an employee to blame all her mistakes on. When that employee left, there was no shortage of employees that would become the next targets. I called it the "fickle finger of fate" that would suddenly be pointing in someone's direction. As an employee you could be doing a great job, minding your own business, only to find out one day she was now your direct supervisor and your career was now doomed. The way management solved this problem was to re-organize and move her out to the field office when she began to directly supervise a long-term incredibly competent and accomplished employee. My co-workers and I all told her she was doomed but she assured us she had the skills to handle this supervisor. Among other things, one of her co-workers ordered millions of dollars of busses but they didn't meet the specifications required in order to have the busses paid for with the grants. Not a small mistake. My friend's career was instantly in turmoil and she ended up leaving and filing a lawsuit. She had the sociopathic supervisor served with the lawsuit at an after hours employee happy hour and the story made front page news when the supervisor doused the process server with her beer. The employee went on to have a very prestigious job and career with a federal government agency.

I managed to dodge the fickle finger of fate for 18 years. Once I was charged with creating a financing district to fund the new federal clean water mandates. This created a new $2 million dollar budget and immediately, the department heads all began fighting over which department head would add this new $2 million dollar program to their kingdom. The arguments and mudslinging went on for months. Having been the person with the most expertise and who created the program, I would have been the most likely choice to oversee the program. But it was split up into three different parts among three different departments with other people managing each part.

Then I was tasked with transferring the $13 million dollar maintenance financing districts from the jurisdiction of the County's Agency to the local government agency where I worked. Oh boy, here we go again. I was busy handling the monumental task of making the transfer happen while the department heads all fought over where this new program belonged. The Landscape Department said it should be there because they do landscape maintenance. Finance said it belonged there because it involved a funding district. The maintenance department said it should be there because they also manage maintenance. While the department representatives were all slinging mud at each other and made each other look bad, I kept a low profile and kept to the tasks at hand to affect the transfer.

I had gotten the paperwork, agenda items and authorizations approved and ready for the Agency Board and the local Council to approve the transfer at their respective formal public meetings. This was no easy task that took months to get all of the bureaucrats from a number of different agencies all on the same page. We were sitting in a conference room discussing the logistics of the approval process when the Risk Manager showed up uninvited. She started at the local agency as an intern and after sleeping with and marrying a department director, rose through the ranks quickly and became…. a department head!!! Her spouse, was one of the leaders in spearheading the disputes over this big new slice of the budget arguing that it should be in his department. Now after all the agencies had reviewed and approved the paperwork, the Risk Manager was demanding an "indemnification clause." Normally this could kill a project or cause significant delays but I was able to get an indemnification clause written, approved through legal and approved by all the bureaucrats involved in TWO WEEKS. This was one of my proudest accomplishments.

When the time came for the program to start, I was in charge of it and I was transferred from Engineering to the Landscape Department. At that time, the Landscape Director had the most pull with the Head manager so he won the war. I managed the program successfully and won at least 15 state and local awards for excellence. After several years, the Landscape Director retired and a new Director was hired. His first week of employment, the Head Manager removed the landscape program from the landscape department and moved it to the finance department where he promoted the finance director to reward him (presumably for his "creative financing.") This in essence removed half of the Landscape Directors budget and responsibility. Shortly thereafter, the Landscape Department had a welcome lunch for the new Director. In his welcome speech, the Director vowed the get the financing districts back.

I thought getting the financing district program back would involve negotiations with the Head Manager. But in actuality, he enlisted his maintenance goons to sabotage me and my program. They would schedule me to give presentations at meetings and then not tell me. Fortunately, the clerical staff gave me a heads up and I threw together one of my saved presentations and did a stellar job. Another time, we had to have a vote of the residents in a small community in order to complete several improvement projects. My staff and I met with the residents and explained the project and it was well received. The landscape goons sabotaged it and went to the newspapers predicting that the vote would fail. Nothing like walking in to work and seeing a newspaper article on your desk about how your project is failing. Well, my staff and I took offense to this and worked extra hard and the project was overwhelmingly approved. My paperwork would go missing from the secretaries in box. But this was no problem because I had already sent her an e-mail with the documents attached. I had a rule of three where any thing I did or any e-mail I sent, I would copy at least two other people, usually the clerical staff. There were very sharp and were on to all of the games. There were so many other examples but it pains me to try to think of and re-live them all. It was about eight years I spent thwarting their petty games.

Then one day I realized, after 18 years at this same government office, the fickle finger of fate was now pointing squarely in my direction. The first thing that happened was I got called on the carpet for improper and excessive internet access. What my supervisor didn't know was that I never filled out the paperwork to be assigned an internet password to access the internet on the employer's secure government network. It couldn't have been me. I could not have accessed the internet. I went to the IT department to see how this happened. I got a printout of the websites that had been visited and I was told that it had to have been done at my terminal. There was about 36 hours of access to sites that included sports gambling, webMD, colleges in England, and European soccer teams. Well there was only one guy with a wife from England (who worked in the Head Manager's office), a college age daughter and ulcers. Over two months he had spent 36 hours sitting at my desk in my private office in a locked department, on my computer. I put a nanny-cam in my office but by then the only thing I got was one employee going into my office and going through my files.

Then, some documents I prepared for the local Council agenda had been altered after I wrote them and I was called on the carpet for the inaccuracies. Well, I kept copies of every version of every document I generated. I kept the copies on my hard drive and not in the main system files so that they would not be confused with the newer versions. (From years of experience, inevitably, the subsequent revisions would require me to put back much of the information that was previously deleted on earlier versions and saving all versions kept me from doing the same work over and over).

When these things happened and nothing was done about it, I saw the writing on the wall and considered my options. I was very angry that my long-time career was being destroyed and there wasn't much I could do about it. I filed a lawsuit (which I won) and I left employment.

It was a great time for me to be off work because my children were competing in high school and college sports and I got to attend all their games which I would not have been able to do otherwise as my previous employment required me to attend numerous night meetings each week.

After four years, my two children had left home and when I saw the job posting for a large government property office, I thought it was right up my alley. It paid less than what I was making but I welcomed the opportunity to be a lower level employee with a job where you work independently out of the fray of the office politics.

In 2009, I started this new job that had a one year training program. I was one of 3,000 applicants, of which the people who scored in the top 10 percent of an entrance exam went on to interviews and of those 25, including me, were selected. During the training program the 25 trainees were assigned to the office in downtown Los Angeles. I felt well during the training program that included several temporary transfers out to the district office. I had perfect attendance and I passed all of the required tests, assignments and licensing exam at the end of training.

After the training program, the trainees were disbursed out permanently to the five district offices. I was assigned to the district office in an industrial area in the high desert north of Los Angeles. Within the first few months of being in the district office, I had a sinus infection. The notes from the doctor indicate that I already had it for a few weeks before I went to the doctor who prescribed some antibiotics. In February, March and April, I was on antibiotics four times but the sinus infection never went away. The fourth antibiotic was a penicillin derivative and I was concerned of being allergic to it so they prescribed prednisone and a fifth antibiotic.

Two days after discontinuing the penicillin based antibiotic and taking the prednisone, I went into anaphylactic shock/syncope with loss of consciousness in my car, while I was driving. I had driven to Hollywood to get a souvenir hat for my niece. Saturday morning I drove my supersize Tundra quad cab pick-up truck on the Los Angeles freeways, past all of the sight seers on Hollywood Boulevard and Sunset. I drove my boat of a truck up a steep driveway into a parking garage up and down the aisles past a lot of high end vehicles and found a parking spot. I did my shopping and got in the truck to leave. I circled through the garage towards the parking garage exit and barrier arms. My left hand slipped off the wheel and jammed against the frame of the car. The pain was so unbelievably excruciating. That was the last thing I remember before I came to with my truck wedged in between two pilasters located by the barrier arms. I had minor damage to the front and rear ends of my truck. If I had lost consciousness earlier, I could have had a serious high speed accident on the freeway, or hit a high volume of pedestrians that mobbed the streets of Hollywood, or taken out a large number of expensive high end vehicles in the parking garage. If it happened a few seconds later, the truck would have rolled down the steep exit driveway and crashed through the lobby into the building across the street.

I give credit to my guardian angels that I was strapped safely in my car seat and had minimal damage to my vehicle when this happened. If I had not been in my car and had lost consciousness when I was walking or standing, I most likely would have had some type of pain or injuries. When you are 6'-3", your head is just a few inches lower than the top of a door frame and any fall is a long way down. I also likely could have landed on a coffee table or piece of furniture if I fell at home or could have fallen down the stairs or on an escalator at the stores I went to. All of these could have had very serious outcomes. After I regained consciousness, I was taken by ambulance to the emergency room. The LAPD officer who took the report made sure they tested me for drugs and alcohol which were NOT present.

Initially it was called a "syncope" and attributed to an allergic reaction to the penicillin based antibiotic. But that theory was questioned. How could I have had a reaction to the antibiotics on Saturday when the last time I took the antibiotics on Wednesday evening? I had previously taken other similar antibiotics with no reaction, why did I have a syncope reaction to this one? If the problem was not from penicillin based antibiotics, could it been from the prednisone steroids or the infection?

This was not the first time my guardian angels had come through for me in a big way. In 1994, we owned a minivan but because it was low on gas, I drove our white pick-up truck to an appointment. I had been driving leisurely home on the freeway when a semi trailer truck on the overpass above me lost a load of 12 inch diameter, two ton pipes that came bouncing down onto the freeway below. I heard the pipes bouncing off the pavement before I saw what happened. One of the pipes speared into the minivan in the lane next to my little white pick-up truck fatally de-capitating the driver in front of my eyes. The pipe skewered into the minivan, opened the roof like a can opener and caused it to rollover. One of the pipes whipped around a smashed in the entire front of my truck and as my truck spun around, I had a 360 degree view of the van in the lane next to me being skewered and rolling over. A second pipe speared through the passenger side of my truck and shot out the back window, slid along the Dura liner and blew out the back gate on the truck bed. If I had driven our minivan or not had the Dura liner lining in the bed of my truck, or if I was a fraction of a second in any direction, I would have been killed. Instead, I walked away with hardly a scratch. I had to credit divine intervention with being in such a profoundly serious situation, and being so un-harmed.

Once again, in the parking garage in Hollywood, I survived a serious situation with hardly a scratch. But, it just so happens that when you lose consciousness while driving a car, they suspend your license. This was problematic because having a valid driver's license was a condition of my employment. I had to go to my supervisor and explain the situation. He met with the higher-ups and they advised me they modified my schedule to include only office work until I got my license back. Fortunately, through another series of miraculous events, I was able to get a note right away from the doctor that prescribed me the penicillin based antibiotics indicating the penicillin allergy caused the "syncope".

At the doctor's office, there was a nurse there whose daughter played on the same volleyball team as my daughter and she wrote me a note on the spot. I went in person to the DMV hearing office and was able to schedule a hearing within a few days. I passed the impromptu written DMV exam without being afforded the opportunity to study ahead of time and passed the DMV road test. Within a week I had my license back. If that's not a miracle to get a letter from the Doctor right away saying that I had an allergic reaction to the antibiotics they gave me, go through the California Department of Motor Vehicles (DMV) system with a suspended license, get a hearing date and get my license back in a week, then I don't know what is.

Several months later, I had a kidney infection; I was on antibiotics several times but could not get rid of it. Ultrasounds and exams with scopes up the urinary tract etc could not identify any specific problems. I was given super antibiotic shots once a day for three days and I was good to go, but only for a few more weeks. In the summer months the office where I worked was very cold. I was told the new district Office

Manager had the AC cranked up to increase production. Presumably if the office is too warm, employees become lethargic. In order to make the AC so cold, the fresh air intakes were closed. This continually re-circulated the same air and caused the air to become dirty and stale. In the winter months, the heat was not working from October until February. I put a thermometer in my cubicle. First thing in the morning the temperature in the high desert of the Los Angeles area, would be between 40 and 50 degrees. By noon the temperature might go up to the 60's from all of the space heaters that were running.

I could not run a space heater from my cubicle. If I did, the circuit would blow and everyone's computers would shut down and there would be audible groans as everyone lost their data. It was pretty embarrassing the first time this happened and I was singled out as the reason everyone lost their computer work.

It doesn't rain much in southern California but when there was a heavy rain in the winter rainy season, the office ceiling leaked badly. At least six buckets had to be set in one of the interior offices next to my desk to collect the dripping water. I stayed back during lunch to help empty the buckets out during the lunch hour if they got full and spilled over.

At the time I was there, the air filters that were only to be used a maximum of 90 days had been used for ten months. I would later be told that the maintenance managers made an intentional decision to decrease the frequency of replacing the HVAC air filters to save money. I also discovered that the fresh air intake had been broken and the roof, pipes, toilets and HVAC system all leaked.

By the time I had reached the point where I had blood in my urine, a kidney infection, daily nose bleeds, ear infections in both ears, a sinus infection and various other problems, it was my husband that suggested perhaps the problem was from mold. I was skeptical at first and wondered, can mold really do this?

I went to work the next day and looked carefully. I saw stains all over the ceiling tiles, there were stains on the carpet. They would clean the carpet but the stains would come back. The women's bathroom that I used on the second floor near my cubicle smelled like mold. I looked carefully at the floor, walls, under the sink and the ceiling. The most notable possible source of the smell was the fuzzy black dirt covering the second vent at the back of the bathroom. The second floor had always had a moth problem and recently had ant infestations. Didn't moths only live in areas of high humidity? The only place I had ever seen moths indoors was in the Midwest. I have never before or since seen moths in any building in California.

I checked my prescription records. I discovered that each time I was temporarily transferred to that office, I was on antibiotics. Then after being assigned to that office permanently, I had been on antibiotics 20 times in the first year. I had not had any antibiotics the year before I started working there.

There was one of the supervisors that had been out sick for an extended period of time and had a Worker's Comp claim. There were other people with symptoms and mold was suspected. But no surprise, the building maintenance manager claimed there was no mold. I wondered, how I could determine whether there actually was mold there? I looked on line. There were companies that wanted hundreds or thousands of dollars to do testing and the various types of tests there were. For my initial testing, I chose the $10 test kit from a local hardware store. I made sure to follow the directions exactly and swabbed the black fuzzy stuff on the bathroom air vent. It seemed like it should be dry dust on the vent but actually was soft spongy black stuff. The directions said to wait 48 hours to see if anything grew. Sure enough the petri dish had black fuzzy stuff growing in it. I unsealed and opened up the petri dish to get a better photo of it before I sent it off to the lab.

Within an hour I had a bloody nose just from opening the petri dish long enough to snap a photo with my phone. I sent the culture off to the lab with $40 to get the test results. Sure enough, it came back indicating six different types of mold (fungus). The report explained that each type of fungus had some species that were problematic and some species that were not. So I needed to know if this was innocuous mold or problematic species. I called the Lab and asked if they could do a species identification. For an extra $50, I got an updated report with species identification. The species included Aspergillus fumigatus and Cladosporium cladisporiodes, Eppicoccum nigrum and Uloladium chartarum. A quick search on the internet indicated the first two of these species are especially problematic as they can infect and colonize inside the body.

It would be nine months later and I would have gone to over twenty different doctors before I found a doctor that confirmed what I already knew: That I had an Aspergillus infection in my sinuses. I would always be told that Aspergillus infections were rare and that I couldn't possible have one. But because of all of the surgery, scar tissue and poor blood supply in my sinuses and the fact that I was prescribed oral and spray steroids, the integrity of my mucous membranes in my sinuses was horribly compromised. But, I found a doctor with an endoscopic camera that went up my nose and took photos and video of the fungal infection and fungal sinusitis.

And so my journey begins: I know there is disease causing mold in the building, now I need to find out if it is the cause of my malady of health problems. My symptoms included:

> Massive Headaches 24/7 from the roof on my mouth
> to the top of my head
> Daily Nose Bleeds
> Kidney infections and blood red urine
> Ear infections in both ears
> Fluid and ear aches in both ears
> Irritability and dizziness
> Swelling of lips, hands and legs
> Weight gain
> Fatigue
> Cramping
> Blurred vision
> Nausea

One of the best online resources for mold and biotoxin illness is Dr. Shoemaker's websites survivingmold.com and chronicneurotoxins. com. There is an online questionnaire and visual contract sensitivity (VCS) vision screening test as a preliminary screen to determine if you are being affected by neurotoxins. Neurotoxins are neurologic poisons produced by the fungus. Snake venom and poison ivy are also neurotoxins. Dr. Shoemaker's website has more details on the VCS test. It's no surprise, I tested positive for biotoxin illness. With other possible causes for biotoxin exposure ruled out through extensive medical and blood tests, it appeared that my exposure was from mold. A urine test was also positive for the mycotoxin produced by Aspergillus.

I purchased and read Dr. Shoemaker's books "Surviving Mold" and "Mold Warriors" that were a wealth of information.

Dr. Shoemaker's books explain how mold spores are everywhere but Water Damaged Buildings (WDB) have high concentrations of toxic molds. WDB's are structures that have had 1) Un-remediated water intrusion from leaks or broken pipes, and 2) People are sick from being in the building.

There are over 100,000 different kinds of mold. As many as 250,000 spores can fit on the head of a pin. Molds produce mycotoxins, which are toxic chemicals that inhibit the growth of competing organisms. Mycotoxins can be 1) Pathogenic – Infection or illness causing, 2) Toxinogenic – Disease causing, 3) Carcinogenic – Death causing. Mycotoxins are biological poisons like rattlesnake venom and poison ivy. Statistically, around 75% of the population is generally not affected by mold. 25% is affected by mold and a percentage of those are genetically unable to process the mold toxins out of their system. People become sickened by inhaling the mold or mycotoxins and any area of the body can be affected by reactions from inhaled mold or mycotoxins.

Exposure to WDB's creates an acute, chronic, systemic, inflammatory illness named by Dr. Shoemaker as CIRS: Chronic Inflammatory Response Syndrome. This inflammatory response can create a myriad of symptoms.

A friend of mine worked at a doctor's office and had said that her doctor's other office had mold problems when a pipe burst and the office flooded. She believed that the Doctor knew how to treat mold. I scheduled an appointment.

The Doctor confirmed what Dr. Shoemaker's website said that if you are experiencing a mold illness, step one is to remove yourself from the moldy environment. I was happy for her support of this very basic step. For some people, this is all the cure they need to recover from mold exposure. However, additional blood tests showed I had mycotoxins in my urine, the same mycotoxins that are made by Aspergillus. The doctor also prescribed the medication Dr. Shoemaker mentions in his books and websites called Cholestyramine. This medication is typically used to lower cholesterol but has the added benefit of being ionically charged and attaches to toxins in the intestines and safely allows the toxins to be absorbed and eliminated naturally through the intestinal tract. Dr. Shoemaker's books and website had a lot of information on how and why Cholestyramine is used on mold patients.

Having been familiar with being in a moldy building, my doctor I went to was totally supportive of not returning to work in the moldy environment. The doctor wrote me a note and I started the Cholestyramine (CSM). The information I read indicated that some people are better after a few days of CSM but others may need it for a few weeks or longer. I noticed a very distinct, gradual improvement of my symptoms. I had excruciating pain in my sinuses, face and forehead and the areas of pain shrank each day from the CSM until it was generally gone. But after I had been on CSM for two months, the pain immediately flared up as soon as stopped or cut back on the CSM, so I knew I still had some type of problem.

In general, I still felt absolutely horrible. I was still fatigued. Half the time when I went for my regular doctor visits, I left the doctor's office before I saw the doctor because I felt so awful or I wasn't even well enough to go at all. My children had bought me a gift certificate for a massage and I made an appointment. I had blood in my urine that day and I felt so bad, I got up and left in the middle of the massage and headed over to urgent care. The massage therapist was offended, she took it personally.

I had a hard time accomplishing minor tasks. I needed to get a prescription, mail my monthly disability note to my employer and then go for an MRI. I headed off to the pharmacy, but when I tried to pay for the prescriptions I realized I forgot my wallet so I went home to get it. Then back to the pharmacy and on to the post office. I pulled up to the drop off box but realized I didn't have the note I needed to mail. So I went back home to get the letter. Then I headed off to the MRI office. Halfway there I realized I forgot to go back past the post office and mail the letter. I headed directly to the MRI office but I went to the wrong place. I got the correct address and had the MRI. I went home and then realized I still hadn't mailed the letter which I eventually did the next day. Three simple things and it took me all day to only do two of them.

One day I felt well enough I wanted to try some retail therapy and buy myself a new shirt. Some of my old ones didn't fit well since I had gained a few pounds. Since I'm 6'-3" tall there are very few stores where I can go in to try extra-long pants or extra-large size 13 shoes on so I was going to settle for buying a shirt. I went to one of the few stores I knew of that might have things I could try on. After trying on almost everything in the store in my size, I found a top that I thought might be OK. I asked the sales clerk if it looked OK. She suggested maybe it would look OK if I wore it with jeans and if I DIDN'T WEAR IT BACKWARDS.

One of the doctors I went to gave me a sinus rinse kit. This was immensely helpful. I have an aversion to spraying stuff up my nose, but the sinus rinse was so soothing and gentle. The instructions say to use distilled water and add a packet of some type of saline mix to adjust the pH of the water. You put it in the microwave to gently warm it up to body temperature and it was incredibly soothing and helpful. During this flushing, I noticed all types and colors of mucous coming out. The sinus swabs the doctors had previously done had all come back negative for fungus. I was told this was not surprising for a number of reasons: 1) they don't use the right growth medium for fungus, 2) the swab may not get to the place where the fungus is, 3) they don't culture for the additional length of time required for fungus and 4) they may only test for a limited type of things. I noticed a disclaimer in one of my negative sinus culture result reports that put limitations on what was tested for and how the testing was done.

I had the idea to collect the multi colors of mucous I flushed from my sinus rinse in a glass bowl, and put it on one of the hardware store home mold test kits. I covered the petri dish and waited 48 hours. Sure enough there was a substantial mold growth and I sent it off to the lab.

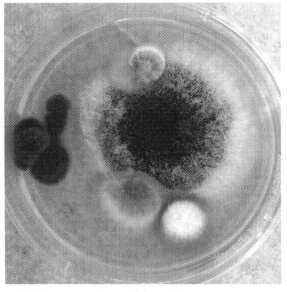

Photo: Petri Dish Sinus Culture
You can see the effect of the mycotoxins, invisible toxins
that surround and separate the different species of mold to
prevent the other species from invading their territory.

The report identified three species, two of which were Cladosporium Cladisporiodes and Aspergillus fumigatus. In the photo, you can see invisible boundaries between the different types of fungus and how the different fungus don't grow into each other. Fungi produce mycotoxins to protect itself and its territory from being invaded by other species. There are 250,000 different species of mold, yet two months after I left the office building, my sinuses still had the same two species of fungus in it that were in the office building. I found this to be a little more than coincidental. The fungus had set up residence in my sinuses and was producing poisonous mycotoxins in my body 24 hours a day, seven days a week. The mycotoxins were permeating my tissues and caused massive pain and headaches. Also, the fungus and mycotoxins drained down the back of my throat in the post nasal drip and got into my stomach and Eustachian tubes.

I wanted to make sure to leave no stone unturned so I went to any doctor I could that was in any way familiar with mold or fungus. I researched anything I could that would help with my problem. At the time I had been to about ten different allergists, ENT's, Urgent Cares etc. and they all had one thing in common. They all mentioned or indicated a concern about litigation in treating mold problems and with treating me if that's what I had. I kept thinking to myself, why are they thinking I am going to sue them, but later on I came to realize, I was not the threat they were afraid of.

While in was at a Doctor's office in another state, a doctor told me that around ten years ago, there was a flood of mold cases in the courts, some of which had precedent setting awards and included detailed science and testing that proved the causation. The State of California and the Insurance companies realized that many of the State, Government and private buildings were full of mold and that the treatment of mold was a huge liability for the insurance companies and the government so there was a decision to deny that mold existed or caused health problems and to put all of the doctors and labs that treated mold patients out of business. That is what I was told by a doctor.

A quick search of the internet for California mold toxicologists shows a doctor who is no longer in business after having had his license revoked for various paperwork violations such as improper record keeping and overbilling. Really? I wish my doctors could be charged with overbilling. There are doctors who kill people or remove the wrong body parts. Isn't that a bigger problem? My impression is that they made this guy the poster child for doctors that treat mold patients and that all my doctors were not afraid of me, they were afraid of losing their licenses.

The political aspect of treating mold/fungal problems is reinforced when you go the CDC website and look up Aspergillosis. One of the concerns of the CDC is "Defining the Public Health Burden". (This statement has since been re-worded to "decreasing the public health burden). The concern is not curing fungal infection or caring about the people with this problem, it is how much this problem will burden the health system and finances of the insurance companies. This really clued me in to the fact that I was going to have a serious battle getting the proper treatment and getting any legal justice. I was now out of work for several months. In spite of having two doctors write letters indicating that my fungal infection was from the office, my workers comp claim was denied and I had not received any disability pay or medical reimbursements. From then on, I referred to my problem as a fungal infection and I refrained from using the word "mold" or mentioning to treating doctors that I had been exposed to mold. **MOLD really was a four-letter word.**

One of the next doctors I went to was an environmental toxicologist (now deceased) in Sierra Madre. I provided him with medical records on my chronic infections and illnesses. He did an extensive number of tests that quantified the effects of the neurotoxins in my body and brain. The toxins affect the brains balance, cognitive functions, vision, memory, mental health etc. He wrote a fabulous report outlining the problems and concluding that I was totally disabled at that time and that it was not known if it would be permanent and it was more probable than not that it was due to mold from the workplace. The symptoms I had at that time were:

> HEADACHES/MIGRAINES – Major migraine pain from the roof of my mouth to the top of my forehead. My teeth hurt and my cheekbones hurt. Area of pain shrank following treatment with CSM. Headache pain 24/7 in the front part of the top of my head 24/7 to current. Pressure in the skull & back of neck.

> NAUSEA - Headache hurts so much I feel like I want to throw up. Scratchy throat, hoarse voice. General feeling of feeling REALLY BAD. It doesn't kill you, it just makes you wish you were dead.

> EYES/VISION – Blurred Vision, started wearing readers, went to eye doctor. Burning eyes. Pain behind eyes with sinus pain and headaches.

> BRAIN FOG, MEMORY LOSS – Difficulty thinking, poor memory. Poor decision making.

> SINUSES – Sneezing fits. Monthly Sinus infections during exposure, no sinus infection without exposure.

Massive allergic inflammation. Sinus infections did not clear up with one or several doses of antibiotics. Burning in Sinuses. Had to continually flush with sinus rinse but burning came back. Voice sounded very congested. After 2 months of being out of WDB, people commented I was sounding better.

NOSEBLEEDS - Daily nosebleeds during exposure. No nosebleeds without exposure. Nosebleeds within 5 to 15 minutes of re-exposure in a WDB.

EARS – Ear infections in both ears for over a month. Fluid in both ears for over a month. Major Loss of hearing. Very LOUD tinnitus. So loud it wakes me up in the morning. Earaches for months to current. Pressure problems in ears.

FATIGUE – Major fatigue and exhaustion problem. My husband called me a zombie. After one month of CSM treatment, can function until noon or 1:00, then seriously fatigued.

CRAMPING – Cramps in calves and arches of feet

INSOMNIA – Problem falling asleep and staying asleep. Wake up early in the morning due to pain in sinuses, headache and LOUD Tinnitus.

MAJOR GASTROINTESTINAL DISTRESS – Noticed this problem after working in building for 6 months.

IRRITABILITY & DIZZINESS – Two episodes of syncope/anaphylactic shock.

SWELLING – Swollen lips. Major swelling in knees, hands and legs after taking prednisone and oral steroids.

WEIGHT GAIN – Gained 20 pounds in six months, then gained another 15. Gained 35 pounds total.

KIDNEY/BLADDER INFECTIONS – Frequent, unexplained Blood in urine. Urine comes out blood red.

HAIR LOSS – Periods of noticeable hair loss and rash in hair at back of head.

DEPRESSION – Upset over career being ruined. Upset over problems not being diagnosed. Don't know what's wrong. Can't find Doctors. Problems with employer and worker's comp. General feeling of feeling REALLY BAD. It doesn't kill you, it just makes you wish you were dead.

I began to have nosebleeds whenever I went into any commercial building that had visible water stains or odors. This phenomenon has been called Chronic Inflammatory Response (CIRS). I took me a while to connect the nose bleeds to the fact that I had just gone into a random store or building. I tested this theory by going back to a building where I had gotten a nosebleed and sure enough within a little bit of time, I got another nose bleed. Just to be sure, I went back several more times to several places and proved that theory. These nose bleeds were not just a little bit of blood getting blown out onto a tissue. This was streams of blood running out of both nostrils onto my clothes and inside my car. It necessitated going home immediately to wash and change my clothes and to take a shower to wash off any allergens that may have gotten on me.

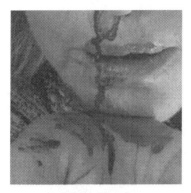

Nose Bleed

Typical blood red urine sample

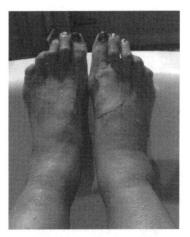

Swollen feet and ankles

The Sierra Madre doctor's Toxicologist report was essential to explain the problems I was having and to establish that the disability was work related and to enable me to get time off of work. However, whenever I stopped doing the sinus rinses and CSM, the sinus pain and headaches immediately became progressively worse. My do-it-yourself petri dish sinus test kits kept showing fungus and I kept getting bloody noses. I believed I had a fungal sinus infection and I needed to determine how to treat it. I kept going to doctors and they either did not know how to treat this or they would not believe I actually had a fungal sinus infection. I asked them to refer me to someone but the referrals went nowhere. The doctors I was referred to did not treat mold patients.

Dr. Shoemaker's website had a list of blood tests he uses to diagnose mold illness patients. In lieu of going to New Jersey to see Dr. Shoemaker, I printed out the list and set out to find a doctor who could review them and recommend those or other tests. The local doctors never heard of the tests, would not prescribe them or if I did get a prescription, the lab didn't do them. There was also another local toxicologist, that I went to who had a list of other tests that were important. It took several weeks of diligence and some techniques that I am not at liberty to share to get prescriptions and lab codes and a lab that would do most of the tests. Sure enough, as doctor Shoemaker had explained in his book, a number of my test results were seriously off. My MSH was low. This is a problem because MSH is what keeps mucous membranes healthy and resistant to infection. This creates a downward spiral where the mold makes MSH drop and low MSH opens the door for more fungal infection that lowers MSH more.

My TGFBeta-1 was 11,360 and should be less than 2,380. In Dr. Shoemaker's book, he says that a patient immediately gets his sympathy when their MMP-9 that should be less than 584 is over 600. Mine was 1,004. I have a three page single spaced list of abnormal test results. The lab tests indicated that I now had ammonia and carbon monoxide in my blood. The toxicologist explained that when mold and mold toxins are metabolized in the body, some of the by-products of this metabolization are Ammonia and Carbon monoxide. She said, I don't care who you are or what the acceptable range is, you should not have ammonia in your blood. I also did poorly on a pulmonary function test and was diagnosed with COPD. Usually, only smokers get COPD or people with chemical exposures. The toxicologist also checked my mouth and sinuses under a black light because some types of fungus fluoresce. Sure enough, the scar inside my mouth glowed. Three years ago I was playing entire games of basketball and now I can't make it up the stairs without gasping for breath after being sickened by mold and toxins. That mold is some bad S#★T!

Antifungal medications taken by mouth or intravenously have been likened to fungal chemotherapy. They are very toxic to the liver and kidneys. The fungal cells are very similar to human cells so that in the process of killing fungal cells, the antifungals kill a lot of the human cells. Doctors routinely require Complete Blood Count tests (CBC's) and tests for liver enzymes prior to prescribing anti-fungals to make sure the patient can tolerate the medications. I had a chance to chat with one of the few mold patients I ever ran into at one of the doctors. She had taken a bunch of anti-fungal medication and now she was on the liver transplant list.

Two doctors did the standard nasal cultures and they came back negative for fungus. The cultures done during my kidney infections had also come back negative for fungus. I was becoming very skeptical of the accuracy of these tests. I finally took one of my petri dish sinus cultures to the doctor's office. I stuck the swab directly in the fungus in the petri dish and paid $200 on my credit card to have the swab cultured through the doctor's regular medical lab. It came back negative! I wanted my money back! I took my petri dish and hardware store mold test kit lab test results to a local ENT to convince him I actually had a fungal problem. He said he had never seen that type of lab report but he prescribed Itraconazole antifungal to be sprayed by nebulizer in my sinuses for 30 days. I did this religiously. I felt better during the treatment but as soon as the meds ran out, the pain and sinus problems gradually returned.

I had read in Dr. Shaller's book, "Mold Illness and Mold Remediation Made Simple" and Dr. Shoemakers books that Itraconazole did not work on some patients with Aspergillus and that they successfully used a Voriconazole spray. My doctors were reluctant to prescribe this. I got one doctor to write me a prescription for oral voriconazole. Apparently, it is very toxic and some of my doctors cautioned against using it. I could never find a pharmacy or lab that had it. One of the doctors I went to looked it up and it costs $10,000 for each of two treatments. The side effects listed on line included inability to urinate. I decided that I would rather have the symptoms that I had than inability to urinate. An ENT agreed that he would prescribe voriconazole spray if I could find a place to obtain it. I couldn't. One of the books mentioned a Doctor in a nearby state who prescribed a voriconazole compound sinus spray for his patients. I called his office to inquire where his patients got that prescription filled. I was told they didn't know where the patients got the medication. I did manage to get a doctor and pharmacist to agree that another medication could possibly be effective so I tried that for two weeks but it was less effective in my sinuses than the itraconazole. This was a little discouraging to say the least.

During this time, I read a book called "Mold: The War Within" written by Kurt and Lee Ann Billings that were affected by mold after hurricane Katrina. Katrina was what really put the problems with Mold on the map. These people had a number of herbs, vitamins and supplements they used that seemed to help them. I tried almost all of their suggestions that included various vitamins, herbs, protocols and recommendations. I found their story very interesting and helpful.

But, I still had the same problem, when I stopped taking the vitamins, herbs supplements, sinus rinses etc, my condition would quickly deteriorate. The fungal infection was still there. It was still making mycotoxins 24 hours a day, seven days a week and poisoning me and my tissues.

One of the next things I did was go to a Mold Treatment Center (MTC) in another state (the center has since closed). Prior to going there, they required a couple more lab tests. They confirmed the presence of fungus, yeast and Ochratoxin, the toxin produced by Aspergillus, in my urine. They did a physical exam and pointed out the white scaly stuff on my feet and heels. I showed them my medical reports and photos of the various rashes that I had on my scalp and body.

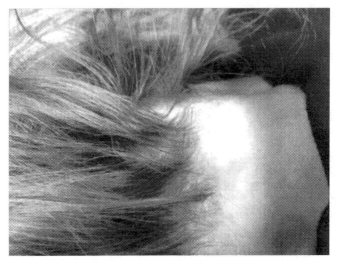

Rash on scalp

For me, they determined that the fungus and yeast becomes systemic in the respiratory and digestive systems. They prescribed a treatment protocol that included taking diflucan followed by Itraconazole. The diflucan is used to kill the yeast and then the itraconazole comes in batting clean-up to eradicate any other fungus in the digestive system. At the same time, medication is taken by nebulizer into the lungs to kill whatever is there and sprayed into the sinuses to kill whatever is there. During the month long treatment process I questioned the doctors whether the Itraconazole was actually going to kill aspergillus or not. I was assured it would but I was doubtful. The CDC website indicates the use of voriconazole to kill aspergillus. Two pharmacists told me that Itraconazole would not kill aspergillus but the mold treatment center and another doctor I would see in the future both provided me with a cut sheet that said Itraconazole would kill aspergillus. I put my faith in the doctors and followed the treatment protocol to the letter. If this plan did not work, I wasn't going to be blamed for it because I missed a dose or something.

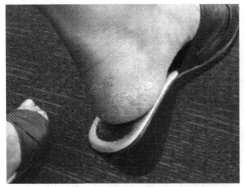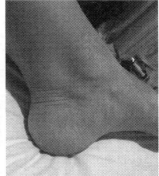

White scaly fungus on
feet before MTC

New pink skin
after MTC

I was happy to see the improvement in the skin on my feet and I did feel better while doing the treatment. But I was absolutely, emotionally devastated at the end of my 30 day treatment protocol when my symptoms began to return. Further research on line showed that Itraconazole will inhibit the growth of Aspergillus, but not kill it. The facial and sinus pain came back. I kept getting nose bleeds within fifteen minutes to an hour of when I was in a moldy building or exposed to mold. After getting the nosebleeds, I would then be really sick for four days. Dr. Shoemaker has called this phenomenon a Chronic Inflammatory Response Syndrome (CIRS). His book explains how MSH plummets after re-exposure and TGFBeta-1 and VEGF spiral out of control. I can't say exactly how TGFBeta-1 or these other abnormal blood tests present in the body but I know that you feel absolutely awful. I was sick in bed for days and weeks unable to do anything but get up and go to the bathroom. At first I was worried that I might die. Then, I felt so bad I had the thought I just wanted to die. Then I started to have thoughts about how to expedite that process. When the facial and sinus pain flared up, it was so painful I just wanted to kill myself. I knew my fungal sinus problem was still there. After the MTC protocol, I felt well enough to go on trip to Yosemite with my husband. During this trip, I developed a rash on the tops of my feet. It took a year to properly diagnose and treat this rash and another four years to be completely rid of it.

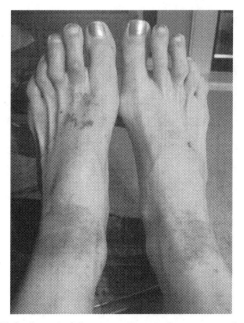

Wicked, painful, aggressive rashes on my feet

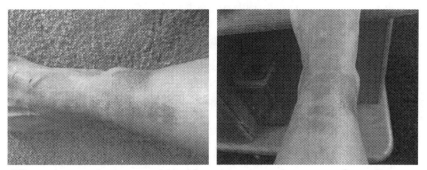

The rash spread up my ankles after a sugar scrub as part of a pedicure

Two of the 25 doctor's offices I visited gave me bloody noses. I would start feeling sick and getting headaches while in the waiting room. As I looked around, I saw black fuzzy stuff on the air vents on the ceilings in the waiting rooms and stains on the ceiling tiles. A few times I felt so bad I went home before I even saw the doctor. Eventually I figured out the nose bleeds I experienced within an hour after leaving the doctor's office was from the dirty air and mold there. The one doctor let me test her office and I wrote a report. One of my do-it-yourself sinus rinse petri dish mold tests done on my sinuses after

I had been in the doctor's office but prior to my testing the doctor's office had two of the same mold species as the doctor's office. This told me that my sinuses had had already been contaminated with mold from the doctor's office before I even knew what types of fungus was in the doctor's office. While I was obtaining the samples from her air vents I started feeling scratchiness in my throat even though I was wearing a breathing mask. I raced home and threw my clothes in the washing machine and I jumped in the shower. I flushed my mouth and throat out in the shower spray. I had a bloody nose before I was done showering. But it was too late. I was already starting to feel the Chronic Inflammatory Response that caused me to feel sick and made my energy level plummet. That was the last time I went to that doctor's office. I started saving the bloody nose tissues in baggies and noting the places that I went that day.

One of my used tissues that grew black mold in the baggie

Eventually, I was able to narrow down which buildings made me sick. I also wanted the tissues as proof of the bloody noses and I knew that they would contain whatever organisms were present in my nose at the time. I was concerned that after I was well, the doctors, lawyers or whoever would claim that I didn't have bloody noses or mold in my sinuses. Later on, I noticed that some of the baggies had black mold growing in them!

The rash on the tops of my feet was wickedly painful, extremely aggressive and itchy. I looked on line. What popped up was that rashes on the tops of the feet can be indicative of systemic fungal problems but there was no indication of what to do. I first went to a local dermatologist who declared that I had eczema and she prescribed a medication. I did not agree with this diagnosis. I could not believe that after 50 years of never having skin problems that I now had eczema. The cream did not work and in fact made it worse. Ultimately, I went to my favorite urgent care and was prescribed ketoconazole, loprox and several other creams. Many of the creams made it worse, did nothing or at best, kept the rash from getting worse. For now, I had a wicked, painful, itchy rash on my feet and a serious problem with my sinuses that no one had treatment for. I decided to go back to my favorite doctor from at the local government run facility.

The look of horror on the doctor's face spoke volumes as she told me that typically fungal sinus infections are treated with surgery to scrape out the fungus and steroids. She said that frequently the fungus grows back in spite of surgery. She arranged for an immediate appointment to see an ENT with a famous local medical facility. The implications of someone with a cleft palate and sinus full of scar tissue having a fungal sinus infection were not good. The doctor mentioned the two "S" words: Surgery & Steroids. One of the Doctors I had gone to said that treating fungal infections with steroids was like throwing gasoline on a fire. I was concerned about going to doctors that treated fungal infections with steroids but for now, I was out of other options. The doctor sprayed my sinuses with anesthetic, looked up there with a camera, did a sinus swab and ordered a CT scan. In the camera she saw three white spots and the lab test of the swab confirmed the spots were Aspergillus infection but I was horrified by the standard treatment she suggested, surgery and steroids.

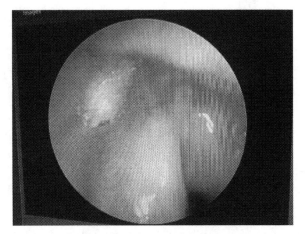

White spot - Fungal infection

Dr. Shoemaker was adamant in his books: "Never take steroids by mouth unless threatened with death" and I whole heartedly believe him. I wasn't sure if steroids used in surgery was part of his admonition. Prior to reading his opinion, I had been prescribed and took prednisone, a steroid to counteract the allergic reaction to the penicillin based drug that seemed to make my lips tingle and swell a little. That was when I had anaphylaxis, could this be a coincidence? I also passed out in a doctor's office when I was getting a cortisone (steroid) shot in my shoulder for the torn rotator cuff. Coincidence? I had also been warned by the last surgeon to never have any more sinus surgery due to the lack of blood supply. So here I was being told to do something I had sworn I would never do. I looked up fungal sinus infections on line. The various websites had two bits of information that stuck out in my mind.

1) There were no antifungal drugs on the market that were reliably effective against Aspergillus and
2) If the Aspergillus infection becomes invasive, the mortality rate is greater than 50%. However, I could never find a definition of when it is considered to be invasive and when it isn't.

Around this time, there was a nationwide fungal meningitis outbreak where a number of people died. A compounding pharmacy distributed some medications that had been contaminated with the same types of fungus, Aspergillus, that was in my sinus and people were dying from the fungus. The medication the fungus was living in: **Steroids!** If fungus can live in steroids, no wonder Dr. Shoemaker finds that fungus patients must avoid steroids at all costs. He says it is like throwing gasoline on a fire. First the steroids suppress the immune system and then it feeds the fungus. Evidently the mainstream medical profession hasn't figured this out yet. For sure, I wasn't going to take steroids so I started writing on all my future medical questionnaires that I was allergic to steroids.

So in the two bits of information I gleaned from the websites, I focused on one word: **drugs**. If there were no reliable **drugs** that killed fungus, were there other substances that would kill fungus?

I had noticed that one of the sprays I got from the treatment center had silver in it. I started researching colloidal silver on line. I ran across a test done by ERSL labs where they had a petri dish with Aspergillus in it. They sprayed the Aspergillus with a colloidal silver concentration of 75 ppm 8 times a day and the fungus was DEAD in THREE days! There was also a manual written by a doctor indicating that colloidal silver could be taken orally at a specified dose dialy for two weeks and continued until the Aspergillus infection was gone. This was definitely worth try. I bought colloidal silver, made sure I had a concentration of 75 ppm (In the test, 20 ppm was not strong enough) for spraying in my sinus and I sprayed the crap out of my nose for two weeks. I like the motto that anything worth doing is worth over doing so I was going to launch an all-out assault on the fungus. I also researched anti-fungal herbs and I found a long list on the internet.

From the list I selected several herbs so I took ginger, turmeric and goldenseal. I also had a friend that was a nurse and the holistic office where she works has a lot of doctors and pharmaceutical sales people as patients. I'm thinking, so this is where THEY go to get well. The nurse suggested that I go see a doctor who treats by using intravenous (IV) vitamin and oxygen therapy. I had read on a website that oxygen therapy was one of the things recommended for sinus sufferers and I was already adding citrus sinus drops as an antifungal to my sinus rinse. I had no idea what type of oxygen therapy was suggested but I went to the local doctor recommended by the nurse. It turns out, one of his therapies included ozone. I had heard of using ozone to kill fungus in buildings but I didn't know there was a medical application. Medical grade oxygen is used and energized to create ozone (O3) that is then inhaled or used intravenously. The doctor would never make any claims about whether the O3 or other treatments did anything but there were many cancer patients in his office who had remarkable progress after their traditional cancer treatments failed including a disappearance of their cancer. Their cancer doctors proclaimed they had "spontaneous remissions" or that the cancer was never there.

So for the first two weeks after I was told of the three white spots of fungal infection in my sinuses, I launched my assault. My naturopathic doctor and I called it the "Blitz Krieg" or "all out war."

1) I used a silver nasal spray in my sinuses per the instructions on the box. The colloidal silver in the store comes in a bottle with a spray nozzle that shoots right up into the sinuses and I also periodically applied the silver with a nebulizer.
2) I took colloidal silver by mouth according to the instructions in the manual and on the products.
3) I took Ginger, Goldenseal, Turmeric and garlic as antifungals along with other various supplements recommended by various Chiropractors and Naturopaths.
4) I continued rinsing with sinus rinse from the drug store with the added antifungal drops I purchased on line.
5) I went to the doctor for oxygen therapy/ozone and IV treatments. I breathed the O3 into my sinuses on my Monday appointment and on Monday and Friday I had O3 by IV in addition to the breathing.

Part of the blitz kreig also included treating my mouth. The dentist indicated that my dental pocket depths had increased significantly. The technician admonished me for waiting so long between appointments but in fact I had actually just been there less than 6 months earlier. I also had found two friends who were dealing with mold issues and both of them had lost one or more teeth. So I dipped a periodontal brush in colloidal silver and brushed it between my teeth at night to hopefully kill fungus. I also sprayed the colloidal silver on my teeth following the instructions on the products. At my next check-up, the dentist said my pocket depths were much better. I have the dental records and pocket depth changes as proof.

After the first two weeks and especially after the O3 therapy, I had the feeling the fungus was gone. I was feeling much better and I wanted to see the spots for myself and see if it was getting better or worse. I found an ENT that had a camera that goes up the nose that is hooked to a monitor. The doctor told me two of the spots were gone! He also pointed out the difference between the fungal infection and fungal sinusitis in my sinus photos. The infected area looked like a white patch but the fungal sinusitis has an orangish tint to it.

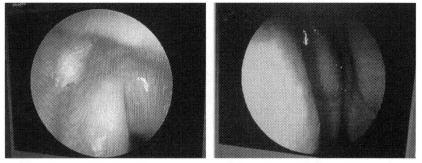

Fungal Infection   **Fungal Sinusitis**

The doctor said the white patch did not have the fuzzy appearance like they usually see but he said that it was probably because of all the spraying I had done. So to summarize: The five steps above made two of the spots go away in a few weeks but the following done during a nine month period did NOT work:

> 10 day prescription of oral diflucan
> 10 day prescription of oral Itraconazole
> 30 day Itraconazole liquid nasal spray by nebulizer
> Cholestyramine (But this was amazingly helpful in removing toxins)
> Various anti-biotics

Steroid nasal sprays
Oral steroids
(taken prior to reading Dr. Shoemaker's book advising
not to take them)

So I kept following the five steps above. I still got periodic bloody noses when exposed to mold or buildings with problematic air quality. I began to pay more attention. Any time I went in a building that had any kind of odor or was dirty or had water stains or dirty vents, I left the building immediately.

I needed some files from my desk at work to process my disability paperwork. My supervisor had the box of my files from my desk delivered to my home. In the box he included some of my personal items from my desk. There was a picture frame and photo from my desk at work and I noticed the picture frame had spongy black dust on it. Within an hour of opening the box, I had a bloody nose. I had an extra hardware store mold test kit and I swabbed the black spongy dust on the picture frame and sent it off to the lab. There were several different kinds of mold on it, one of which was called rhizopus/mucor. I noticed how quickly this fungus spread over petri dish. After the first day, it nearly covered the entire dish. I sealed the box of files and put it outside. I put the box in the bed of my truck and drove it to the vacuum station at the local car wash. I didn't want that stuff in my vacuum cleaner or my house! I vacuumed all the books and papers and wiped them down with wipes. I put the files in plastic bags and put them in a clean box and stored them with my files. One day I was preparing some paperwork and reviewing many of my files including the ones in the bags. I got a bloody nose that day. I'm not sure if it was from the contaminated files or not but I put the files in the garage and I will not be opening those files again without further decontamination.

Fast growing Rhizopus/Mucor, from my work desk picture frame, altered the surface of the entire petri dish after one day

My Employer continued to deny any problems in the building. I wanted more definitive proof that my fungal problem came from the office building. I took my mold test results to OSHA and asked them to inspect the building. I got a copy of the OSHA file after the inspection was done. It was a gold mine of information. While they can't test the building for mold as there are no set standards or limits, they did do an inspection. They interviewed employees who said the building leaked, had poor ventilation and HVAC, and that there were employees that felt sick or unwell or had health problems at work. They required the building owner to provide maintenance records. The records indicated that the building leaked like a sieve since the day it was built. Not only did the roof leak, the pipes, HVAC, sinks, toilets, disposals, etc. chronically leaked as well. The sewer backed up out of the toilet onto the carpet and was remedied by just cleaning the carpet. A lot of maintenance work was NOT done due to "maintenance HOLDS." The maintenance contractors had not been paid and refused to do any more work until they received payment. I found a maintenance proposal saying the regular maintenance had not been done as needed and the equipment was in a state of disrepair and that as a result the maintenance work would be more frequent and extensive.

The OSHA inspector was assured by my employer's building manager that the leaks had been fixed. However, I found a proposal to replace the buildings broken heater that included a line item to fix the oxidized platform on the roof that contributed to the leaks. The heater replacement only was authorized in October of 2011 while I was still a functional person, but the line item to replace the leaky platform was NOT authorized. A copy of the work authorization and payment check confirmed that the leak fix was not included or paid for. The non-functional heater was not fixed until five winter months later, in February 2012, after I was deemed too sick to go back to work on January 29, 2012.

I was bound and determined to have an independent company test the building as the tests I did could be challenged. It could be alleged I did them wrong, or that I was not qualified, or that I misrepresented where the samples came from. My employer had sent me a written letter refusing to allow me to test a proposed work location and refused me to have access to the secure building I had worked at which required keycard access. I was told by the OSHA inspector that not only is the employer supposed to allow an employee to test, that the employer is to take it upon themselves to test if there are problems. Although I worked on the second floor, there was a public lobby and bathroom and I hired a company to surreptitiously go in and test those areas. The mold test found Stachybotrys, toxic black mold, on the baseboards in the lobby and found the same species of Aspergillus that was in my sinuses. The bottom of the public urinal was covered in green slime that was tested and found to have e-coli and fecal coliform in it.

I continued my treatment and hoped for that last infected spot in my sinus to be gone. I was wondering what the spot would look like if it got flushed out in my sinus rinse which I routinely collected in a clear glass dish and examined before discarding. I was wondering if I could save the spot and have it cultured but did not know how to go about this. My problem was solved when I went back to the doctor two months after the three spots were first documented. The ENT was able to use his suction device to remove and capture the spot and send it off to the lab. I anxiously awaited confirmation that this was in fact fungus and what type of fungus it was but somehow, the specimen and the sinus swab never made it to the fungal culture lab.

My dog had been limping for at least six months and he also had a large skin tag at the corner of his eye. At his regular vet check up, the vet was concerned about his limp but I was more concerned about the aesthetics of the growth by his eye and whether it was going to get worse. The vet gave me an estimate of $650 to remove the growth under general anesthesia and gave us some tramadol and prednisone (a steroid) for the dog. After having read all of the warnings against using steroids for fungus because it was like throwing gasoline on a fire, I was reluctant to give the steroids to my dog. I gave him a tablespoon of colloidal silver in his food five days over a one week period and applied a high potency silver product topically. By the end of the week, the growth by his eye crumbled away. I have subsequently run across information about using colloidal silver for skin tags. I love colloidal silver. An on line search for colloidal silver shows the different types of silver products and uses. It is good stuff but the medical doctors will typically never prescribe it or any other over the counter medication to anyone as they are generally trained and licensed to only prescribe pharmaceuticals. A lot of information about vitamins or over the counter medications has disclaimers that state that you should consult with your doctor before taking any of those products. But the truth is, the doctors will never prescribe or recommend those products because they will only talk about prescription medications from pharmaceutical companies.

I went back to the doctor who was the only one to correctly culture the fungal infection a get a result of "Aspergillus" from the special fungal lab. She confirmed the three spots on the left side were gone but that there was another spot on the right side.

I had a lot of intestinal distress. X-Rays at the urgent care showed a lot of retained stool and gas in the intestines. I also had a lot of intestinal cramps, especially at night. My intestines would painfully cramp, cramp, cramp on the left and then painfully cramp, cramp, cramp on the right all night long. I went in for colonic irrigations. It seemed to me that the toxins kept accumulating in my intestines and made them sluggish. I also used Cholestyramine (CSM) once in a while to pull out toxins. While it can be constipating and I always took psyllium capsules also per the CSM instructions (but not taken at the same time) and it actually helped with my constipation. I also took broken cell wall Chlorophyll tablets along with the psyllium as directed in the CSM protocol. This seemed to work well too. I also felt that my intestines were irritated by the massive quantity of herbs I had been taking. I think the chlorophyll was very soothing. It helped the cramping subside a little.

Colon hydrotherapy was suggested by one of the mold websites so I went to see a colon hydrotherapist. In colon hydrotherapy, body temperature water is used to gently flush out the intestinal tract. There are different machines and methods. There is one type of machine that is especially easy and convenient. It also has a clear discharge tube where you can see the waste after it has been flushed out. I could see massive quantities of small and large gas bubbles. I was told this was yeast, also known as a fungus called Candida Albicans. The colon hydrotherapist suggested that I take some anti-yeast products as well as some probiotics. After trying numerous anti-yeast products, I found two anti yeast products that combined, contained a wide variety of most of the antifungal herbs from a comprehensive list I found on line. I also tried many pro-biotics. The colon hydrotherapist had me watch a video on pro-biotics during my session. The video explained that the intestinal tract is the largest immune system fighting organ, making it one powerful force for our health and the fight against illness. With over 400 species of bacteria living inside our intestines, it is very important that we keep the levels of good and bad bacteria in balance. I already knew a lot about pro-biotics but what stuck with me was that there are many pro-biotic organisms and that each one did different things. I had previously tried a popular yogurt 10 day challenge where you are supposed to take the product for 10 days to help your digestive system. After 5 days I had more severe cramps and bloating. I was so upset that I complained to the FDA and the manufacturer. The yogurt commercials were later changed to say that the yogurt makes you feel good and not make any claims of improving digestion. After this problem, I tried to avoid any patented probiotic. I sought out different yogurts, kefirs and capsules to provide the biggest variety of the most different organisms. My favorite is the greek yogurt with live cultures of L. Acidophilus, Bifidus and L. Casei. I also like Kefir. The brands I tried had <u>seven to ten billion CFU's</u> of 10 strains of bacteria, plus alleged clinically proven probiotics. Kefir balances your body's ecosystem and supports digestive health and immunity – that's 12 live and active cultures per cup. I also took a probiotic drink, even though it has a proprietary organism in it. One day, the grocery store was out of the brand I used but had the Spanish equivalent. Initially I was upset about Spanish products being sold in America. But as I read the ingredients, it had five different types of organisms, more types than the American version had, so now I try to buy the Spanish version. I also take a pro-biotic capsule. I have tried a number of them and now I use a brand that had billions of 14 different organisms. I used to just take pro-biotics once a day but with all of the anti-biotics I have had, I try to take one or more types of probiotic with each meal.

While I was healing and feeling better, I was able to get out more and run errands. I frequently found myself having accidently gone into a building with unknown air quality for 15 minutes to an hour and then having nose bleeds shortly thereafter. These would frequently be accompanied by blood in my urine, kidney infection and the typical chronic inflammatory illness that would last four days. I would be so depressed after seeing the bright red blood in my tissue because I knew I had four days of illness coming. (Later on. these bouts would last two to six weeks) I did my best to alleviate or mitigate the symptoms, but I could never escape the symptoms. On days two and three my energy would just be so trashed.

I noticed I had decreased sensitivity in my feet. I couldn't really tell how hot the water in the tub was by sticking my foot in. One day at the grocery store a giant bottle of water fell off the top shelf of the grocery store and landed square on my foot but I didn't really feel anything. I saw it hit squarely on my foot and I thought to myself, wow, if I had feeling in my feet, that's gotta hurt. The pain did come the next day. It was excruciating and lasted for two days and then was suddenly gone.

I bought an ozone machine so I could save money. I could not give myself IV treatments, so I could only breathe it in through my sinuses. You can also drink ozonated water which is not so tasty. Ozone can also be applied to the limbs through the skin by "bagging" them. In my case, I put my feet in an insulated bag to treat the rash and filled it with ozone and treated for the length is time recommended by the ozone manufacturer.

I had eased off on my IV ozone treatments but I noticed a decline in how I felt in spite of breathing it in through the sinus cannulas. I also noticed that for the rash on my feet to have any benefit, I had to do both the IV and bagging ozone treatments. So, I resumed doing the IV treatments approximately twice a week.

I had been struggling with the rash on my feet. I had been to a number of different doctors who suggested a number of different prescription and over the counter creams. These would keep the rash from getting worse but would not make it better. I speculated that the rash might be from Aspergillus. After all that was what was in my sinuses. So I did some research on line. The information confirmed what I had guessed. These antifungals only suppress the growth of aspergillus but don't kill it. I continued with the ozone treatments to try to eradicate the rash. One weekend, I was horrified to find that the wicked, itchy painful rash that I had for the last eight months had suddenly spread from the tops of my feet to my ankles. I was beside myself. Was this going to continue to spread up my legs? I started applying every kind of cream and ointment I had. I applied some of the amphotericin from the vials I used for my sinuses. Wow, this actually seemed to make a difference. It seemed to actually start healing.

After a couple days I realized where the rash had come from and why the rash had suddenly spread. I had a pair of shoes I bought new for walking at work. I used to keep them under my desk at work and I wore them walking every day at lunch rain or shine. Now, I had worn them hiking in Yosemite over the Memorial Day holiday. That was the first weekend I noticed the rash. I wore them with a pair of calf high socks. I wore the shoes again the last weekend. That time I wore them with ankle socks. My feet got rashes in the exact same outline as the shoes. If you note on the photo below, you can see where the rash was under the mesh in the shoe and the new rash area followed a clear cutline above where the sock line was and extended up beneath where the tongue of the shoe rubbed against my foot. What made the rash suddenly spread like wildfire was the sugar scrub that the pedicure ladies had done on my feet. Sugar feeds the fungus.

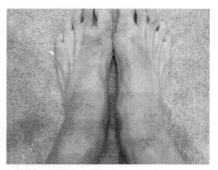

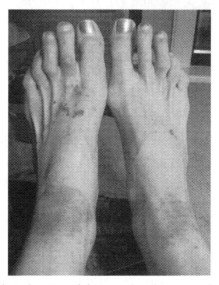

Wicked, Itchy, Painful Fungal rash on my feet from wearing the shoes I kept under my desk at work

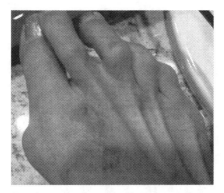

Fungal infection above and Fungus fluorescing under a black light below.

Time for another Mold Test Kit! I got the shoes and immediately took them outside the house. I took one shoe and pressed the tongue of the shoe on the petri dish. When I pulled the shoe off the gel in the petri dish, a layer of gel stuck to the shoe. I was worried that instead of the fungus coming off the shoe into the petri dish, that the gel came out onto the shoe. I took the other shoe and used a sterile knife to scrape the particles of the bottom of the tongue into the petri dish and sent it off to the lab. Within hours, I started feeling very ill and I got a nose bleed. OMG, I must have inhaled some of the particles and spores from scraping the shoe. I jumped in the shower, washed my face, rinsed my mouth and throat etc. I was horrified all over again.

Now, I was worried that the wicked itchy painful rash from my feet was now going to be in my sinuses. I made an appointment with the sinus doctor to see how it looked and to try to do some damage control. In the mean time I did my sinus rinses, colloidal silver sprays and ozone. I also continued using the amphotericin on my feet. I got the results back from my shoe. There were five kinds of fungi including Aspergillus and the same five types of fungi that were also found in the office building. Four of the types of fungi are capable of causing rashes. One of the species was specifically identified to be treatable with amphotericin.

I had an appointment to see a dermatologist. I was hoping to get a biopsy to have an official medical diagnosis for what was causing the rash on my feet. Her office called and cancelled saying she was sick but later on indicated she was leaving for a three week conference the next day and they were cancelling all of the appointments for that day.

I had seven other Dr. appointments that week. I went to see the ENT again. I was worried that she might not want to see me because they would have received the subpoena request from my workers comp case. By then, at least four of my other doctor's so far had indicated they wouldn't see me since they have received a subpoena. So I smiled and was very friendly when she came in and said I was happy with her and the infectious disease doctor she recommended and that I had been asymptomatic before my recent re-exposure. (I actually was NOT happy with the infectious disease doctor because he prescribed 3 months of a prescription that does not actually kill Aspergillus.) She asked me what medication I was taking and I said the Amphotericin nasal spray was working well for me. She asked me what doctor prescribed it and I told her.

She asked me about the infectious disease doctor. I said that what he prescribed did not work and does not kill aspergillus. She railed into me that I needed to stay with the same doctor and not switch around. (My take on this was that their doctors prescribe medication that doesn't work so that surgery is necessitated.) She said "Oh no, you can't use amphotericin! It doesn't work!!" She bagged on the amphotericin saying that it does not work and that it has not been proven to penetrate the skin and that they only use it during surgery. I said that I was using it on my feet because I tried 20 other things and none of them worked except the amphotericin. She said it doesn't work except after surgery when the skin has been opened. My take on this was that it works really well, so well that they don't want people using it because it precludes the need for surgery. That even no matter how the surgery went, the patient would get well because of the amphotericin. She said my sinuses were looking good. I told her about my shoe and my sinuses being exposed to the shoe fungus and she did another culture. I showed her the lab test from my shoe. She said she would call me with the lab results. She referred me to a Dermatologist and to a sinus surgeon. I felt like she was passing me off as a problem patient to a competing medical organization. My naturopathic doctor confirmed, I had been dumped!

And as I suspected, somehow the sinus culture never made it to the fungal lab. It did come back from the regular lab positive for Bacteria: Proteus Mirabilis and CoAg Negative Staph but she didn't think anything needed to be done to treat it because the counts were so low. It was my opinion that the counts were low because of all the sinus rinsing and spraying I was doing.

Dr. Shoemaker has indicated in his book that a lot of mold patients have CoAg negative staff remaining in the sinuses once the fungus is gone. He calls it MARCoNS: Multiple Antibody Resistant CoAg Negative Staff. He indicates that this bacterial surrounds itself in a protective biofilm and is difficult to kill because the antibiotics can't penetrate the film. There is a compounding pharmacy that makes a nasal spray composed of a biofilm busting agent with antibiotics specifically for this purpose. After discussing this with my doctor, he prescribed me with the special nasal spray.

I also read that EDTA can dissolve the biofilm and that baby shampoo contains this substance that can dissolve the biofilm. I also read about someone who had added a couple drops of baby shampoo to their sinus rinse. At first this sounded disgusting but I tried it and the sinus rinse was still soothing and therapeutic.

I noticed that the CDC website had some major updates about mold and fungus. The recommended treatment was voriconazole, which I already knew. But the stuff is really toxic and at the time was expensive. I was told it costs $10,000 for each of two treatments. The only other mold patient that I met at a doctor's office had taken oral anti-fungals and now was on the liver transplant list.

When I was at the dermatologist of a very prominent LA medical center, he was adamant that my foot rash was NOT fungal. I asked him how many Aspergillus patients he had seen. He said he had seen about 13 but they were all in the hospital with their skin falling off. My take on it was that they failed to identify Aspergillus in the earlier stages was why they only saw severe cases.

One of the dermatologists I was referred to was not available so I made another appointment with the first available dermatologist. I ended up seeing a young inexperienced person. I asked for a biopsy but she said "that's not how they do things!" I was adamant I wanted a biopsy but she refused. I tried to show her the lab test report from my shoe and she would not look at it. I was insistent that I was allergic to steroids and said it caused syncope/anaphylaxis. She said while I may be allergic to oral steroids, I probably wasn't allergic to steroid skin creams. She said I had dermatitis and recommended a cream and an over the counter treatment for treating and moisturizing dry skin. I asked if it had steroids in it and she said no. I asked about getting a refill for my prescription for amphotericin that was working and again she said "no, that's not how they do things!" She said that I would absolutely not get better unless I used the cream she was going to prescribe me which turned out to be a steroid and a moisturizer.

In my experience with the rash, the moisturizing creams caused the rash to flare up. That contrasted with the use of oxygen, ozone and calamine lotion products that made the rash dry up and feel better. I looked up the steroid cream on line that she prescribed. It said it was not to be used to treat fungal rashes.

I also had an appointment with an infectious disease doctor. He was insistent on finding out how long I took the Itraconazole. I eventually told him 10 days but he should have already known that was what I told the other doctor who put it in her notes and now it should be in the patient database they all have access to. I was pretty sure he would also have seen notes in the computer indicating that they had received subpoenas for my workers comp case. I asked him about the rash on my feet. He also refused to biopsy it and would not acknowledge that it could be fungal which seemed like something that could be considered since he was treating me for an Aspergillus fungal infection in my sinuses. He did say how odd it was that the rash was exactly the same on both of my feet and in the outline of my shoes. He refused to listen to me try to tell him that it was from my shoes that I kept under my desk at work.

I wanted to ask him why he prescribed Itraconazole (sporanox) for Aspergillus when everything on line that I have seen indicates that Itraconazole does not kill aspergillus, it only inhibits the growth. I also wanted to ask him why he didn't do any liver function tests prior to prescribing me three months of itraconazole. I can't recall if I asked him for a refill of the amphotericin but I was running out. I was using a combination of amphotericin to kill the fungus and calamine products to manage the itching.

I used up all the amphotericin –None of the doctors I saw would re-fill it. I was getting discouraged from trying to get a refill from another doctor. I had just been applying a calamine lotion product. The rash was mostly gone and the calamine seemed to keep what little was left from getting worse. Then one day I was in the drug store and I couldn't believe my eyes. I saw some silver cream!!! OMG, my favorite colloidal silver comes in a cream☺ I started using the silver cream after I ran out of amphotericin and it seemed to do the trick although it seemed to take forever. It also seemed that I had been having a minor spreading of the rash to areas adjacent to the initial rash. It seemed that my pant legs had been rubbing against my legs, spreading the fungus as they rubbed on my legs and getting the fungus on my pants and then re-contaminating my legs if I wore the pants again. So I boiled my pants and I threw the remaining shoes I had into the washing machine. Later on I ended up just throwing the shoes out. I felt like a crazy person boiling my pants and throwing my street shoes in the washer.

I also noticed that I would have the rash mostly gone only to have it flare up suddenly. I realized that the rash was weeping into my slip on shoes that I wore without socks. Months later when I wore the shoes again, the rash would go from the shoes back to my feet. I was later told by a doctor I need to throw out all of my special order size 13 ladies shoes and my expensive special order extra tall clothes that I had worn into work.

As part of the workers comp claim, I was directed to have a sleep study to investigate my claims of sleep problems. I went to the sleep study center that the workers comp doctor scheduled me for. I noticed an odor in the hallway on the way to the sleep study office. Ordinarily, this would have been a clue for me to leave and not come back but I had brought an air filter purification device and I did not notice the odor once I was in the office. I had to place the air purifier on the floor because of the tables were not near the outlets and there was not enough room on the night stands. I was directed to try to sleep on my back as much as possible. There was an air vent directly over the head of the bed that blew air constantly on my face and down my throat all night long. I woke up in the middle of the night with a sore throat and it was worse by morning. The air filter location was generally ineffective because it could not filter the air after it left the vent but before it blew directly into my throat. I had the worst sore throat and felt terrible. Not even well enough to go to the doctor. I did my best to use my sprays and rinses to solve the sore throat problem but to no avail. I went to urgent care for antibiotics. Also purchased some antibiotic nasal spray. I was sick in bed and on and off antibiotics for about five weeks after the sleep study. I thought that I would have gotten a nose bleed to alert me of any problems but I never got one. Then after a few weeks of being infection free, I again had kidney and sinus infections and was antibiotics for another two months. I had discontinued the ozone therapy for financial reasons but I realized that I had was not on antibiotics at all during the time I had the IV ozone treatments so I resumed the ozone.

Workers comp had denied my initial claim because they claimed my illness was not work related. This in spite of the fact that now four of my doctors wrote letters or reports to that effect. After a year I was still not permanent and stable but an appointment was scheduled with an Agreed Medical Examiner (AME) about a year and a half after my last day at work before I went on disability. During that year and a half, I had not received any medical reimbursements or disability pay.

My long term disability (LTD) pay was denied. In order to be eligible, the employee must have been employed for five years or had a work related illness. I had not been there for five years but I provided them with the letters from my four doctors indicating my illness was work-related, from the office building. I also provided them with a two inch binder of tabbed and organized medical records with photos of my fungal infection, a culture from Cedars Sinai indicating the infection was aspergillus and four mold tests from the building showing twenty different kinds of fungus including aspergillus and the toxic black mold: Stachybotrys. They NOW claimed that in order to qualify for a work related illness, my workers comp claim needed to be accepted but this was not in the criteria listed in their informational pamphlet. They denied my appeal.

The doctor who had given me the intravenous ozone suggested trying intravenous vitamin C. His patients have had amazing results with it. I met many of the patients that he was treating who had cancer and traditional cancer treatments hadn't worked or they used it in conjunction with traditional cancer treatments. One patient was a nurse that had stage four cancer. After numerous standard cancer treatments, the doctors gave her two months to live and sent her home to die. Using an intravenous regimen, she is now back to work and has amazingly healthy looking skin. I started using the vitamin C to help heal my sinuses but I noticed that the rash on my feet became less aggressive with the vitamin C. Without using anti-fungal cream, the rash would keep getting worse. In conjunction with the amphotericin to kill the fungus, the vitamin C seemed to help the skin on my feet heal. After a year of having a continuous rash on my feet, the rash was finally gone. I also noticed that my intestinal distress was gone and my intestines started working normally again without laxatives or colonics.

A year and a half after my first day off of work, I got to see the first Agreed Medical Examiner, a doctor agreed upon by my worker's comp attorney and my employer. His report affirmed that he believed my illness was work related. I believe that the only reason he supported this conclusion was because I had also filed a civil suit against the property owner of the office building and that the employer's liability is limited in a worker's comp case. It seemed to me, they were just limiting their liability by accepting the case so that they would not be added as a defendant in the civil case.

I reviewed the report. The report was fraught with errors and there were a number of things that didn't set well with me. On the first page, the doctor indicated that I did not have a college degree, when in fact I do. I felt that here on the first page, he was downgrading my credibility. The most egregious error was the omission of a years' worth of medical records. The records started in 1992 when I gave birth to my daughter. There were dozens of pages of records from the birth of my daughter and over forty pages of records about an injury I had in 2009 with a broken foot. Yet the last accurate medical records about my current problems were dated June 2012, a year before the date of the report, May 2013. A years worth of medical records were missing.

I thought the way the last records were listed was highly suspect also. The June 2012 record was followed by lengthy pages of deposition notes from June of 2012. After the end of all of the useless deposition notes was a record from a doctor dated March of 2013 thereby giving the appearance that the records went all the way to 2013. But I never saw that doctor in 2013. Her office gave me nose bleeds and I quit seeing her in mid-2012. I never got an accurate diagnosis until Sept/Oct of 2012. I also went to several Doctors who had done tests and written letters. None of those tests or results were included.

So to summarize, while the report included extensive details of the gynecological reports from when I gave birth and broke my foot, the report left out the twelve months with all of the important tests and diagnoses from my current illness. The last record was followed with pages of insignificant deposition notes and ended with a bogus medical record dated March 2013 thereby giving the impression that all medical records through that date were included. What I also found highly suspect was the date of the last medical record being around the same time as the deposition. How had the AME doctor received records that only went until June 2012? The AME was selected in October of 2012. If the records were subpoenaed at the time the doctor was selected, the reports would have gone through October of 2012. If the records were subpoenaed sometime close to the appointment date in April of 2013, the records would have gone up to the date the records were subpoenaed. I had made a list of doctors that I had seen in the last ten years for them to use to use for the subpoenas and I had updated that list several times after I saw new physicians. Perhaps they were using an old list? Maybe that would explain it? But no, that couldn't be the answer because I had gone to the local urgent care in the beginning and every month during my illness. They would have provided all the records they had up through the current date, whenever the records were requested. But those records weren't there. Could the AME have used the same records that were subpoenaed by the employer's attorney for my deposition in June 2012? How would doctor have had access to those records?

As a result of the missing records, the AME claimed that he did not have evidence that I had an Aspergillus infection and that I had been disabled but now was able to return to work with no restrictions. Thank goodness I had the persistence to get to a sinus doctor with an endoscopic camera and video screen. I took photos and video of the screen with my cell phone. The video showed the doctor manipulating the camera in my sinus and him explaining about the difference between fungal infection and fungal sinusitis, both of which were present and visible in the video. I also took a photo of the computer screen at the ENT's office that showed the results of the fungal culture showing Aspergillus. They refused to print it out at the doctor's office and I was concerned that if there was litigation involved that the record would disappear. One of the cancer patients I met at the naturopath's office had some of her son's medical records disappear, apparently intentionally. I didn't want that to happen to me. I provided the additional records to my attorney to provide to the AME who issued an updated report. (Later on I discovered that the note indicating the medication had caused me to lose consciousness while driving was no longer in my medical records).

Eventually, I was able to get a copy of the positive fungal sinus culture. I had gone in personally at least three different times to the records department trying to obtain medical records. When I just asked for my medical records, it was not included. When I just asked for my lab test results, it was not included. One day, a helpful clerk indicated there was a special fungal lab and those records had to be specially requested from that lab and were not part of the regular medical records. Then I finally got it, the hard copy of the positive fungal culture.

In reality, what I had written on the questionnaire at the AME's office was that I was still having serious allergic reactions to indoor environments, presumably because they had mold and airbourne particles that caused me to have a reaction. Within 15 minutes to an hour of being in particular buildings, I would get a nose bleed that was followed by an allergic reaction/illness that would last from hours to days.

The following endoscopic photos were taken after the AME report. The red bloody areas and the dark hole should not be there.

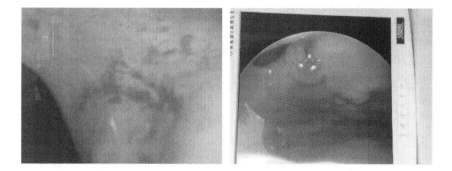

By the fall of 2013, it was over a year and a half since I had left work. I still had bleeding ulcerations in my sinuses and the wicked rash on my feet was back. I was told that by law, I was supposed to receive acceptance of my workers comp claim within 60 days of the AME report dated May 13th, 2013. Since my employer is self-insured, I do not get regular workers comp from the state of California like most everyone in the state would. My employer hires a third party administrator to manage their worker's comp program. The 60 day deadline to accept my case was over on July 12, 2013 with not a word from the third party workers comp company. The calls and letters from me and my attorney were all un-answered.

One of the measures I resorted to was to pray for divine intervention. I did a Novena prayer to Saint Teresa where you say the Novena prayer every day for nine days and at the end of the nine days you have an answer. I had seen a show on TV where some nuns had needed a staircase built. They did the Novena and at the end of the nine days, a traveler had come by and asked to stay at the convent. They agreed he could stay if he built the staircase which he did. I had success with the Novena previously and I tried it again. At the end of nine days, I had a dream that I was trying to get on a train but I didn't have a ticket. In reality, the acceptance of my Long Term Disability benefits, insurance premium reimbursement, disability pay and medical expense reimbursement all hinged on getting the letter accepting my Worker's Comp claim. This was the ticket I needed. So for the month of August, every week, I sent letters and left messages for the Worker's Comp and the employee liason person who manages the WC company contract and sent copies to the attorneys and my HR people. Still no calls back or letters from anyone.

My friends, Doctors and Therapists had suggested that I go to the newspaper with my story. There was recently a story in the paper about a football cornerback at a famous college that had recently had a rare fungal infection that was determined to be an Aspergillus infection. It had spread from his sinuses to his brain. He was fortunate that the college he was at had a famous medical school. He had four surgeries and was in the hospital for a month. He recovered and was able to go back to playing football.

My hat's off to him for his courage and determination. I watched a U-Tube interview and he was asked how the doctors were able to diagnose and treat him. He said "I don't Know", "I was an experiment." That totally sums up the treatment plans I had received from the doctors. They were winging it.

I had concerns about taking my story to the newspapers. This was definitely a big step and once done, there is no going back. I asked to be shown in a dream if this was the right thing to do. I had a dream of being burned all over my body. I certainly didn't want to get burned. This was not the right thing to do. I decided it was the threat of this going public that was going to get some action. How was I going to do this? Call up my employer and demand that I get my benefits or I go to the newspaper? They probably have no clue about my problem.

I had recently won a free Reiki class in a drawing at a bookstore. Reiki is a no touch, hands on healing technique using the life force energy to promote healing. This is the same chi energy involved in Tai Chi, acupuncture, prayer, etc. I thought it couldn't hurt to look into this and possibly get free Reiki healings from the people in the class. I also learned that the Reiki energy could help with problems other than physical healing. As part of the Reiki class, students were supposed to practice it at home for a certain number of sessions to see if they noticed a difference. The reiki instructor had some amazing stories, but I always like to put things like this to the test. Would I notice anything? So I followed the Reiki instructions. I tried using it to heal the issues related to my illness and worker's comp problems. I hoped to have an answer in my dreams. *I previously had the dream about being at the train station and not being able to get on because I didn't have a ticket.* The ticket I needed was the letter accepting my claim. This was holding up everything. Without it, I couldn't get my long term disability, my insurance premium reimbursements, the medical expense reimbursements or disability pay. How was I going to get that acceptance letter? The next morning I went out for a walk. That Saturday morning, out of the blue the idea popped into my head to send the following e-mail:

Attn: HR Manager:

It is my understanding that my worker's comp claim was to be accepted within 60 days of the Agreed Medical Examiner's report dated May 13, 2013 indicating my illness is work related. That 60 days ended on July 12, 2013 and I have not yet received the acceptance letter. Since July 12, 2013:

Calls and letters from me and my attorney have not been answered.

At least three letters and several calls from me to the worker's comp administrator have not been answered:

Two e-mails and two calls to the CEO's office have not been answered.

My attorneys calls to the administrator and their Law Offices have not been answered

My complaint letter to the CEO›s office third party contract administrator has not been answered.

Medical Bills I was directed to send to the administrator are still unpaid and going to collections.

I would like to resolve this through the normal proper channels.

However, the bottom line is I need a copy of the claim acceptance letter.

I need to be reimbursed for my medical expenses. It is URGENT that I be able to pay for and receive my ongoing medical care **in a timely manner** to keep the aggressive infection from getting worse and hopefully to eradicate it completely as soon as possible. I'm sure you are aware that I am being required to provide the acceptance letter in order to receive LTD and other benefits.

What will it take to get this resolved? The details of this issue are explained below.

Employee Battling Deadly Aspergillus Infection

An employee has been battling the same type of deadly Aspergillus sinus infection as the college cornerback reported in a recent newspaper article. While the cornerback's infection spread outside his sinuses, the employee's Aspergillus infections is still contained to the sinuses but after a year and a half, still has not been completely eradicated. Doctor's reports from five doctor's indicate the causation of the fungal infection was the workplace as a result of poor building maintenance and poor indoor air quality. At the time the employee worked at the North office she had sinus infections, kidney infections, ear infections in both ears, nose bleeds and blood in the urine all at the same time. While the head of the agency was arrested for accepting campaign contributions in exchange for tax reductions, the North office was in a state of disrepair. Public records from the OSHA file indicate roof and HVAC leaks, broken fresh air intake, previous allergy and illness complaints, air filters not changed timely, no heat for three months in winter, etc. While quarterly management inspection walk through forms only identify things like tears in carpet, other records show leaking water fountains, toilets and sinks, and the sewer backed up out of the toilet on to the carpet. Some of the leaks and HVAC problems took weeks and months to fix. According to OSHA and ASHRAE, leaks should be fixed within 48 hours to prevent the growth of illness causing organisms. Testing identified the Aspergillus fungus in the building as well as Stachybotrys, Pennicillium, Rhizopus/Mucor, e.coli, coliform and many other organisms that can cause illness such as rashes, respiratory problems, chemical sensitivities and more. The employer's office has not complied with numerous paperwork and response deadlines in processing claims. The Worker's Compensation Board approved a serious and willful misconduct petition against the employer.

I know this may not be your direct responsibility but **Please help me resolve this or direct to the person I need to go to that will answer my calls**.

I would appreciate a copy of the acceptance letter or a call from someone ASAP.

Wow, this was pretty strong. I had concerns about whether to e-mail it or not. I had wondered how I would include language that communicated a concern that they needed to pay attention to me or I could go the newspaper and here it was. I didn't even need to make a threat. The message was clear. These government employees could not care less about my illness and my dire financial situation after not getting any pay for the last year and half or the seriousness of my health problems. The thing they do care about is their career and how they look. This email makes it clear to them how bad the Head Official will look (I'm sure they have been directed to prevent any more bad press about him), about how bad the HR department will look (their reports didn't mention any of the problems), how they can't deny the problem exists because the records are available to the public, and how they can't deny that I'm wrong about the problem because I have records from five doctors. I prayed for an answer about whether to send the e-mail. The first night I had a dream: *about being in a court room and the judge spoke very clearly and accurately. He enunciated everything perfectly.* This seemed like a good answer but I wanted to make sure. The next night I had a dream: *about getting a room full of Christmas presents that I was supposed to get last year.* This seemed like it was a go so I sent the e-mail Monday morning September 9th. By Wednesday 9/11, I got a letter in the mail from the workers comp company indicating that my claim had already been accepted but that my pay would be delayed for a few months while they were waiting for information from the AME. The letter was dated (backdated?) September 6 and the metered stamp on the envelope was September 10th, the day after my e-mail. Unbeknown to me, my civil lawsuit attorney had sent a subpoena to my employer for records and the certification of mailing was dated Sept 9th, the same day as my e-mail. It could have been this subpoena that inspired them to suddenly write a letter indicating my claim was accepted. After all, an accepted worker's comp claim limits their liability in a civil lawsuit. But I find it hard to believe that the subpoena letter would have gotten through the mail room, delivered to someone, and that someone would have had to know that there was a worker's comp case, and to contact the WC company to direct them to accept the case to limit their liability. And of course it could have entirely been a coincidence that after a year of not having any correspondence or responses to calls or letters, they decided to accept my case. After I got the acceptance letter, I had another dream: *There was a long line of people at the train station. A new line opened up and I was first in line. I had a ticket but the clerk needed to go get a claim for my baggage.* About a week later I had another dream: *I was on the train!. I had been on another train and I had left my baggage there. I was asking people about how to get my baggage. Later on I saw it. I was very happy that I got it back.*

Back at the office, the investigation was ongoing into the head official in charge of of my employer, for accepting campaign contributions in exchange for reducing people's property taxes. While I worked there, he had given me a personal letter of glowing recommendation and I had an official photo of the two of us shaking hands in the official office in front of the flags. It wasn't worth much now. There were outside contractors that were part of the scheme. One of the other employees and I had been to the home of one of the contractors to inspect his new multi-million dollar home as part of our regular job duties. Before I had left work, that contractor had been involved in a confidential employee meeting and berated the employee, who was a good friend of mine, for not getting with the program. The employee and his supervisor were outraged. How was this outside contractor allowed to sit in on employee meeting and berate him. Now, the contractor and head of the agency were under investigation and soon would be under arrest.

I was still having problems with nose bleeds after exposure to indoor environments. While I stayed at home or walking outside there were no nose bleeds. My family was going on a European vacation and I opted not to go along. My mother in-law expected that we stay at her hundred year old house in the 900 year old village in North Belgium and my family had made hotel reservations for a trip to Prague and Vienna after they left Belgium. What if I got a nose bleed at my mother-in-laws house? How could I explain I couldn't stay there and had to go to a hotel? What if we got the one of the hotels in Vienna or Prague and I got nose bleeds or was concerned about the hotels and didn't want to stay there? How was I going to have a group of eight relocated to another hotel? What if I got sick and ended up in bed the whole vacation and did not have access to my various medications, therapies and protocols? What if I ended up getting re-infected with the deadly aspergillus fungus? The consequences could be dire. I ended up staying home.

I stayed home alone for ten days and enjoyed my stay-cation. I relaxed and took the dog to the beach. I had a friend Amy who also had mold illness. A review of her HLA DR haplotype indicated she had the "dreaded" genotype that is multi-susceptible to molds, chemicals, toxins etc. People with this genotype have extra difficulty eliminating toxins from their bodies. She also had a friend Pam that she was concerned about. Her friend was having health issues. Amy always got headaches and symptoms at Pam's house. Pam had also previously had mold exposure issues but believed that her house was OK. But, sure enough when I went to Pam's house, I got a nose bleed. I invited Amy & Pam and their dogs over for a few days to help Pam get out of the house and into a clean environment for a while. I had previously tested my house and it had a very low spore count. I also have some high powered air purification machines running to super clean the air. After all, if it's worth doing, it's worth over doing. I was going for spore counts of zero. While they were visiting, we all piled into my giant tundra quad cab and went out on a few trips. One day we drove five miles to the center of Newhall to see the Buffalos at Hart Park in the middle of the Santa Clarita Valley.

While they were there, we took a trip to several hardware stores. When I got back from the hardware stores, I had a nose bleed. I have previously been in two of the stores with no nose bleeds. I couldn't remember if I had been in the third store before or not. Could it have been the third store that gave me the nose bleed? The next day we went to visit her brother at the VA hospital. I was afraid to go in the hospital for fear of being exposed to any microbes that my weakened immune system couldn't handle. On the way home we stopped at a local Mexican restaurant and by the time we got home I had a nose bleed. The next day we just hung out around the house and in the evening they packed up to leave. We gave each other hugs out by the car and they drove away to leave. By the time I walked back in the house, I had a nose bleed. I re-evaluated my nose bleeds from the last three days. They all happened after we were all in the car together. I believe the nose bleeds were from being in the car with Pam, that her clothes and person had high levels of fungus or mycotoxins from her house and that these caused me to have an inflammatory response. I did not experience symptoms in my house because of the massive air filtration devices, but when we all went out in the car, I got the nose bleeds. Believe me, it doesn't go over well when you try to tell someone they can't bring their friend over anymore because their clothes give you nose bleeds. This resulted in a round of nasty texts and e-mails.

A few weeks later, my friend Amy and I went to a book fair at a property that was formerly an old estate of a famous movie director from a previous era. Amy came by the night before and we drove together the next day. There was a massage room and I paid for both of us to get massages. While waiting for my massage my eyes scanned the room as I was now accustomed to doing. I looked for ceiling leaks and water stains in the floor or carpet. I did not see any obvious problems. There was a fan blowing into the massage area and they had a cloth they put over your eyes while doing the massage. Usually, they will use a tissue underneath the cloth but in this case they didn't. We drove back to my house. By the time my friend drove away to go home, she had a massive nose bleed. She was very quick to blame my house for her massive nose bleed. She was pissed at me for causing problems with her friend who did not take it well at all that I accused Pam and her house of giving me nose bleeds. But after talking about it, we came to the conclusion that although I didn't get a nose bleed, we both were experiencing problems from the massage room. It was either the air in this small out building on this old estate or perhaps the eye cloth that had been placed directly over our eyes and nose had been exposed to mold.

The next weekend I went to two tile stores. My husband wanted to rip out the flooring in the master bathroom but I didn't want him to start ripping out until we had the new tile picked. I got nose bleeds from both tile stores. It could be there was a lot of particulates in the air from the tile dust.

I had previously been managing my sinus problem and it was basically pain free and I was just using amphotericin spray to try to eliminate the bleeding ulcerations. My nebulizer for spraying my sinuses with Amphotericin had broken. I was prescribed Amphotericin in a spray bottle from a different pharmacy. That was handy, I just needed to use a simple spray bottle instead of messing with the nebulizer. With all these new exposures, the pain, swelling and inflammation flared up. The severe headaches, pain in my cheeks, forehead, sinuses, the roof of my mouth and bridge of my nose had all come back and seemed to spread like wild fire. The recent lab tests came back indicating the presence of cladosporium and past or present systemic candida. I started amping up my protocols. I used the sinus rinse more frequently. I added silver sinus spray to the amphotericin spray. I used benedryl at night as my one doctor suggested to improve sinus congestion and to help sleep. Nothing seemed to be helping very quickly. I started breathing the ozone in my sinuses again. These all helped but the improvement was slow. I was concerned that either 1) I had been re-infected with fungus or 2) the infection I had had gotten worse and spread. Why wasn't the amphotericin working? Do I need a different kind of nasal spray like voriconazole? Do I need to take the oral antifungal sporanox again? What is happening?

I made an appointment with the ENT to look at my sinuses again endoscopically but the soonest appointment with the fungal ENT with the camera scope and TV screen that I could get was a month away. What doctor could I possibly go to in the mean time to get any answers? It was hard enough to get a prescription for sporanox when I had lab reports and photos of the infection. I showed the doctor the bottle of Amphotericin that I was using and he said it had been compounded using dextrose (sugar, food that fungus thrives on). The doctor said that dextrose on a fungal infection is like throwing gasoline on a fire. The amphotericin nasal spray with dextrose that I had been prescribed had made the infection spread like wild fire. I was prescribed a new nebulizer and more Amphotericin without dextrose. I added colloidal silver by mouth again and added that to my protocols. After the first day, it seemed that this was definitely helpful. The pain in the bridge of my nose, cheeks and sinuses was almost gone. I could still feel pressure and swelling but it was way better. The head ache in my forehead was not gone but was much less than the day before. I re-read all of the literature I had on it.

At this time, I was also making a concerted effort to get the rash on my feet to heal. I went to the local Doc-In-The-Box and I was lucky to get an experienced and knowledgeable doctor. He looked at the foot rash and likened it to the "jungle rot" rashes he had seen the Vets come back from Viet Nam with. He said it was difficult to get rid of and that some people never get rid of it, that it may be something you just have to live with. I told him I also had the fungal infection in my sinuses. He re-iterated what I already knew. He said I needed to keep the fungal infections and rash under control and that if it spread into my brain or became systemic, I could die from it. The rash on my feet kept spreading from my feet into the inside of my socks and shoes and then back to my feet. This recontamination prevented the rash from healing. The doctor suggested shoes that wouldn't re-contaminate my feet. It was no easy task to find some special shoes for my men's size thirteen feet that would fit the bill. The only shoes I could find were these ill-fitting size twelve pink sparkle shoes. They were even on sale. But I have to tell you, I'm not a pink sparkle kind of person.

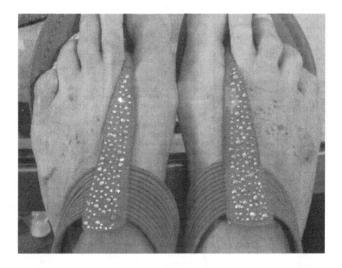

Because of my concern over the flare up of my sinuses, I also started going back for Intra Venous Vitamin C. It seemed that the next day, the inflammation of the rash on my feet just seemed much better. The rash looked very much the same but the fire had gone out of it and it just felt better. But after wearing the shoes every day for a month while applying the amphotericin two or more times a day along with IV vitamin C and applying some Calamine products to help keep down the horrible itching, the wicked jungle rot rash that I had for over a year and half was finally, completely GONE!

It took a total of four months of Amphotericin every day to get rid of the rash. Hopefully, all I needed to do was spray it in my sinuses for four months and then my sinuses would be clear. The warm moist sinuses however, are not as easy to clear up as dry exposed skin. I focused on spraying the Amphotericin in my sinuses religiously.

At this point I would like to summarize a few of the medical records from various doctors:

I have COPD

I don't have COPD

I have asthma

I don't have asthma

I have MCS - multiple chemical sensitivity

I don't have MCS

I have allergies

I don't have allergies

I don't have my tonsils

I do have my tonsils (They've never been removed. I don't know where they went)

I'm a smoker

I'm not a smoker (Really, I've never smoked)

I had someone else records in my workers comp file that said they had an STD

I'm a male (no really I'm female)

So you see how getting well can be a little confusing?

My doctor's reports said I had chronic and recurrent fungal, bacterial and viral infections of the eyes, ears, sinuses, throat and urinary tract. My eyes would get infected and would not clear up with a regular course of antibiotic treatments. I had numerous trips to the eye doctor each month and purchased various pharmaceutical and over the counter eye drops, eye sprays and eye wipes. I had to go to the emergency room twice because my eyes were so infected my corneas got scratched and I couldn't open my eyes.

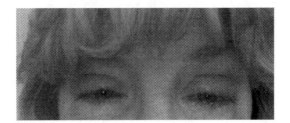

I could barely open my eyes while they were infected

My chronic sinus infections and UTI's would not clear up with regular antibiotics so I had repeated visits to the ENT and urologist and ended up with a variety of prescription and over the counter treatments for sinuses and UTI's. Eventually I had to go in for daily antibiotic shots or IV antibiotics. I also had thrush, shingles and several bouts of pneumonia. The shingles pain was a walk in the park compared to the wicked, evil pain of the fungal rashes. I had accumulated quite a collection of sore throat lozenges and sprays, sinus sprays and rinses, remedies for intestinal distress, etc. I also had a lot of antifungal products for doing laundry and cleaning. I had antifungal toothpaste and mouthwash. I also had various air filters and products such as a spray to keep the air clean and knock mold spores out of the air. A cheap and easy way DIY air filtration device to filter a lot of air very fast and cheap is to buy a box fan and tape a 20" x 20" air filter to the back of it.

I was supposed to start receiving disability pay within 30 days after the AME's report dated May 2013. That didn't happen. I filed fraud complaints against the third party administrator for delays in handling my claim. In January 2014, my worker's comp case was changed to be handled by a different third party administrator. They sent me a letter telling me who the claims examiner was. I sent them copies of records from the seven doctors and two medical examiners that indicated my illness was work related. A few weeks later I got a letter saying I was eligible for permanent disability benefits and that they "will continue to pay for medical bills." They hadn't paid for any so far but I re-sent them a bunch of bills. No response. I continued to send certified letters. If the jurisdiction of the governmental agency I worked for was a separate country, it would be among the 20 largest economies in the world. I was not just fighting with a worker's comp system, I was fighting an entity the size of a country.

I traveled from my home in California to the East Coast to see a fungal sinusitis expert I was referred to. Of course, at the time I went I was between flare-ups so the doctor was unable to see it at its worst. He advised me I needed to avoid all re-exposures to environments that had mold or fungus. He said I should throw out any clothes and shoes that I wore into the work environment. I had worn some of my work clothes into his office and he tested them. He told me how to test my home and auto. I used the test plates from the lab he recommended. The instructions said to expose the test plates to the air in each room for one hour and the random mold spores would land on the plates. Then you would send them for analysis. It was best to achieve a mold count of between 0 to 2 spores. A worst case scenario was a spore count of TNC: Too Numerous to Count. In order for me to get well and stay well, I needed to live and work in environments with a spore count of between zero and two. My home and auto tested between 0 to 3 spores and the spores were not from problematic species. This validated that my home was not the original source of my fungal problems.

The doctor did a blood test that indicated I had low growth hormone. He said growth hormone is what helps regenerate new cells and the lack of it can prevent healing. He sent me to an endocrinologist for more detailed growth hormone testing. The endocrinologist explained the reactions I was having to moldy environments. When the body senses the presence of organisms that previously caused illness, it sends out attack cells. But fungal cells are similar to human cells and so the attack cells attack the human cells in addition to fungal cells. Then the human cells sense more attacks and send out more attack cells and so on. The way I understood it, it was like the war scene in the Matthew Broderick movie "War Games". As in the movie, I called this reaction: 'Global Thermonuclear War.' He also advised me to have a specialized test done at a hospital which required blood draws every half hour for six hours. When I went for the test, usually they do one needle stick to start and IV and then draw blood out of this same needle stick every half hour as required. However, they could not get the first needles stick started so they needed to start a new blood draw each half hour. A lot of time no blood came out so they had to re-stick numerous times for each draw. Then it took twenty minutes to get enough blood out. They missed a couple of the blood draw times because it took so long to find a vein and get blood out. The results came back OK on that test. I would not need to have regular growth hormone shots. But I now had an understanding of the illness that came on so fast after a mold exposure. It was 'Global Thermonuclear War.'

In the mean time, I had a deposition and a mediation in my Civil Lawsuit against the building owner. The defense counsel was willing to acknowledge that I had a fungal infection but they were going to use the "Some Other Dude Did It" defense. They were going to claim I got my infection somewhere else. I felt it was important to do more testing in the building to establish that was where I got the infection. I was previously denied access to the building and was only able to have an inspector go into the lobby. My attorney issued a subpoena to test the building. I knew that some work had been done after OSHA gave them a punch list but I was certain it wasn't enough to fix all the problems. I was concerned that another major clean-up would be done that would eradicate a lot of evidence, although I was certain they would not be able to clean it up well enough to where my inspectors couldn't find historic fungal evidence. I had my inspector go into the lobby again. He said he had some new testing methods. This test showed 85% of the fungal spores found were Aspergillus, the same organisms found in my sinuses. The percentages of indoor spores should roughly mirror the outdoor percentages. Typical percentages of outdoor counts in California have about 35% Pennicillium and Aspergillus combined. This 85% of Aspergillus only was clearly in excess of any outdoor limits and indicated active or previously active mold growth. Also, 50% of the spores were Group 1 molds that are only found in water damaged buildings, that can damage buildings and cause health problems. The levels of Tricothecene mycotoxin was 2.551 ppb, in excess of the threshold of 0.2 ppb. Tricothecene is a mycotoxin usually associated with Stachybotys, a mold that was previously detected by my mold testing company on the baseboards in the lobby. Stachybotrys is a heavy sticky fungus that requires large quantities of water for extended periods of time to grow and is usually not found in air samples. But here it was, far away from any obvious source of water. The inspectors report indicated a condition 2 mold condition existed in the building. Condition 2 is an indoor environment that is primarily contaminated with settled spores that were dispersed directly or indirectly from a condition 3 area. A condition 3 area is an indoor environment that is contaminated with the presence of actual mold growth and associated spores. Actual growth includes growth that is active or dormant, visible or hidden. Eureka! The report validated my claims and supported the claim that my sinuses became infected from that building.

After OSHA's inspection and my receipt of the maintenance records in September 2012, I had submitted another complaint that there was no evidence in the records that the roof leaks had ever been fixed. The OSHA records clearly showed the owner, staff and employees knew the roof leaked and water dripped into the offices but a thorough review of the large quantity of documents included in the maintenance records did not show any repairs to the leaking platform or the roof. I went to the local Building and Safety office to see if there were permits for fixing the roof. Not surprisingly, there was nothing about any roof repairs as this can possibly be done without a permit. But what was surprising was that they did NOT pull a permit for the $34,000 pressure boiler vessel (heater) they installed on the roof. I filed a complaint with building and safety about the work being done without a permit. Some building and safety departments would have been all over that. They could have charged double fees to the owner for this lack of compliance and obtained the additional permit and inspection fees. But the local building office did not care about this and referred me to the Contractors State License Board where I filed a complaint. What do you know, within a short period of time, I went back to the building and safety office and a permit for the boiler had now been pulled. I had previously taken a series of photos over several weeks in Oct of 2012 of the roof after it rained that showed water ponding on the roof that stayed for in excess of 48 hours, in violation of OSHA standards. It was really easy to take photos of the flat roof on top of the two story building. There was a hill at the backside of the building and across the street in front was a condo project on another hill, both giving me excellent vantage points for observation and photos. I wanted to see if I could tell what the corroded platform looked like. Was it possible to see the corrosion and leaks? The photos I took from 2012 and 2014 are shown below:

ROOF PHOTOS:

10/2012   7/4/2014

I wasn't able to see any particular problems with the platform but I was shocked to see a fresh coating of leak repair and sealant on the roof in 2014. This was two years after the building manager had told the OSHA inspector that the leaks had already been fixed. Some of the buckets of leak repair and sealant had been left on the roof and I was able to zoom in and see what kinds of products they used. We had submitted another subpoena for repair records and the information we got still did not include the roof repairs.

Fresh white sealant/paint   Buckets of sealant and
at all pipes and wires   roof repair left on roof

I searched the County Superior Court website for previous litigation that the building owner was involved in. It appears that when the building was originally built, he hired people or companies with undocumented workers and then he wouldn't pay them. The undocumented workers got together and hired a labor lawyer. The companies and the undocumented workers filed liens and lawsuits. A lot of times the construction worked stopped and new companies were hired to come and finish the jobs.

The building owner's property manager was deposed as part of the legal process in my civil lawsuit. His testimony was basically that if there was a way to save money, defer costs or do something cheaper, that's how the building owner did it.

It was August of 2014. I was seriously aggravated because I still had not received a dime of worker's comp money, medical insurance reimbursement etc. The mandatory workers comp settlement conferences in February and May were continued until the Workers Comp Court date in August and that got continued until October.

Time to work on more divine intervention. I had been praying the Novena to Saint Teresa that I had prayed throughout my life and I usually got an answer to my questions at the end of the nine day prayer. This prayer had worked for me a number of times but this time I felt I was not getting an answer. I also had been doing some I AM decree type of prayers to St. Germain which had usually worked for me in the past. If you do the decrees/prayers for 5 to 15 minutes, three times a day, by the fourth day you have an answer. These prayers had previously been successful but now these weren't working. The only answer I got was to wait for divine timing. I felt like my government employer was a giant immovable object that couldn't be influenced. One day on August 29, 2015 after I got word of my August Court date being postponed, I had an idea to pray to Ganesh, the remover of obstacles. I was raised as a Christian but I honor most all paths of religion as I feel they all point to God. I went on line to find a prayer to Ganesh. I was shocked to find that that day, August 29th, was the first day of the annual celebration to Ganesh and you could offer prayers to Ganesh for each of the days of the festival but I wasn't certain for how many days. What are the odds of that? I read about Ganesh as a symbol for an aspect of God. I can't find the exact language but I read something about the divine energy being like and elephant blasting into a situation and trampling the problems and obstacles to pieces. That sounded good to me. So that day I said the prayer and mailed a copy of the prayer along with an offering to Sai Baba's Ashram in India.

The prayer was:

> **Salutations to the supreme Lord Ganesha**, whose being shines like a million suns and showers his blessings on everyone. Oh my lord of lords Ganesha, kindly remove all obstacles, always and forever from all my activities and endeavors...... including my efforts to........

I did the prayers every day. My bank accounts were drained from paying for medical treatment and my finances were incredibly low. One day I was not feeling especially well and wanted to treat myself to a cup of coffee at the Starbucks drive through. A frantic man in a black luxury car looked pleadingly at me to allow him to cut in front of him even though I was clearly there first. I had nothing urgent I needed to do besides go home and do a sinus rinse so I didn't think anything of letting him go first. He paid for my coffee before he left the drive through in front of me. I was so grateful for this little financial and emotional boost. Then, I received by mail, a gas card rebate from a credit account balance. I had money for gas! Then the incredibly incompetent staff of the back east doctor's office I had been dealing with since March called me now in September at 6:30 in the morning California time saying they finally were able to properly bill the insurance company (after my five calls and letters) and they were refunding my $25. I had been keeping an eye on my bank balance because I was worried that the check I sent to Sai Baba's Ashram in India as an offering wouldn't clear the bank since my accounts were all drained by now. By the last day of September, the check had still not cashed and my bank balance was $12.43. I knew that I was to get an automatic deposit the next day. I was upset I didn't have enough money for the check if it came in that day. If it hadn't come in now, what were the odds that it would come in THAT day? Late that night I checked my account again to see if my deposit was in yet. But to my shock, the check had come in but amazingly it was paid even though my deposit hasn't come in yet. A previous automatic transfer had put money into the maxed-out overdraft protection account and there was enough to cover the check. That night I had a dream: *I was on a plane and the flight attendant was telling me how bad the illnesses from mold can be. Then the pilot banked the plane steeply, flew under an overpass and came in for a quick, steep landing on a freeway.* I felt the dream had to do with my fungal issues and that the trip I was on was coming to a quick end. THE NEXT DAY, I got the worker's comp stipulation and award letter in the mail from my attorney for me to sign. Once I signed the document it would then be signed by the judge and I would get awarded my disability pay! The next day after the STIP came, I received some sacred ash from Sai Baba's Ashram in India in response to my donation. What amazing timing. I should receive the disability pay within 20 days after the judge signs the STIP. Now that my case had been accepted by Worker's Comp, I wanted to see what I needed to do during the open enrollment period so I didn't lose my medical insurance. In the past I would send letter after letter and call after call with no answer. Now I got an answer within a week.

My sinus symptoms had flared up in October after I had been to several buildings where I got runny noses upon entering the buildings. When the disability retirement people called me, I was able to truthfully say that my sinuses were nearly swollen shut. If you looked at my nose with the naked eye, my nostrils were just slits instead of round nostrils. My ear drums were swollen and full of fluid. The doctor looked at them and said Holy S#!* your ear drums look like they're going to explode. I later looked at the medical report wondering what the medical code for exploding eardrum was. All it said was "swollen tympanic membrane."

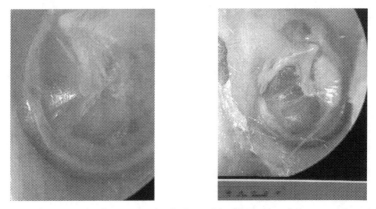

Photos of my normal ear on the left and bulging eardrum on the right

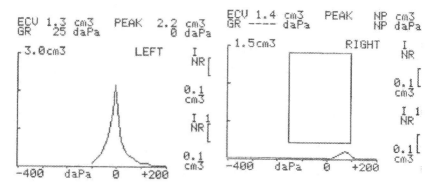

Copies of ear drum pressure tests showing the normal left
ear drum graph and the abnormal right eardrum graph
showing the damaged ear drum cannot hold pressure. I also
lost a significant amount of hearing in my right ear.

That weekend, I saw on TV that the college cornerback that also had an Aspergillus infection in his sinuses was back playing football and he scored the game winning touch down. I was jealous that he was well and I wasn't. But he had all the resources of his colleges medical staff at his disposal, he was twenty years old while I had just turned fifty five and I had a sinus full of scar tissue from my cleft lip & palate surgeries. He was able to obtain voriconazole tablets and I still hadn't found a pharmacy I could get them from except for a pharmacist in another Country.

The deadline for my employer to pay me the disability pay was 30 days after the court date or November 6th. The deadline came and went. I called my attorney and filed fraud complaints. In December, I got two of the three payments I was supposed to receive. I received a lump sum for permanent disability damages and back disability pay for a year. I did not receive any of the medical expense reimbursements.

I had been fairly free from flare ups for a number of months but during those months I had very low blood pressure. My blood pressure had always been one of the few of my medical tests that had still always been normal, always around 120/70 but now it was down to 79/47. When it was that low, I could hardly walk or see. There were always discussions at the doctor's office about whether I should go to the ER or if they should call an ambulance. At the doctor's office they had me eat salty pretzels until my blood pressure went up enough to where I could drive home. There is no medication for raising blood pressure.

By the end of December, I had flu-like symptoms. By January I was diagnosed with pneumonia treated by antibiotics followed by a sinus infection with treated with two courses of antibiotics followed by a urinary tract infection and peeing blood, all the while continuing the amphotericin antifungal nasal spray by nebulizer.

The fungal sinusitis doctor who I considered to be the best expert recommended breathing oxygen and wrote me a prescription. I found that if I breathed the portable oxygen through a nasal cannula and went into a building that had previously given me a nosebleed, that I would NOT get a nosebleed or even get any symptoms.

As a child growing up and until my mold exposure illness, my medical tests would always be normal. I could have been sicker than a dog with flu or getting pre-op lab work or whatever and the tests never showed anything out of normal. Now, no matter what tests were done, it was routine for them to be abnormal. My blood pressure and EKG were now abnormal. When I had the lung x-ray that showed the pneumonia it once again showed the tennis ball sized pericardial cyst attached to the right side of my heart first noticed five years ago when I had an MRI for a back injury. I had it evaluated by a specialist at that time who indicated it was asymptomatic. A CT scan was done and the exact measurements of the cyst were noted and I was told to have it re-evaluated annually. That problem had taken a back burner since all my time and resources had been devoted to killing deadly fungus and dealing with my chronic infections. With this showing up again in my chest x-ray for pneumonia, they strongly urged me at this time to see a specialist again and referred me to a local heart doctor.

I made an appointment with the heart doctor but had to postpone it because I was too sick to go that day. On the re-scheduled date, I showed up with my previous CT scan, a photo of the cysts from the scan and two abnormal EKGs (along with a previous normal EKG prior to mold exposure to compare the changes) hoping to get an order for my annual CT scan to monitor any changes. The doctor did not speak English that well. An ultrasound was done along with another EKG. While I was lying on the table getting the ultrasound, I looked up at the ceiling directly over me and was horrified when I realized the vent above my face was covered with thick black stuff. The holes were completely covered with the stuff. The doctor said the ultrasound was OK but was confused by the different EKGs and then looked at the old one and told me my EKG was normal. I had already looked at it before the doctor came in and I knew it wasn't normal at the present time. Then the doctor told me that because the cyst was outside the heart it was outside the area of her expertise and refused to give me an order for another CT scan. My whole reason for going there was to get the order. I was furious but kept myself under control. Shortly after I left the doctor's office I got a pain in my sinus. It was suffering from an allergic/inflammatory reaction to her dirty vents and took over six weeks to clear up.

I kept telling my therapist the up-side was I didn't get angry with the doctor and I did not get arrested for assaulting her and that the police were not called as they were in a previous incident.

As a child, I had braces on my teeth on and off from about age five to high school years including on my baby teeth because of the cleft lip and palate and subsequent severe misalignment of teeth. About ten years ago I had gone to an orthodontist for aligners to fine tune the straightening of my teeth where I paid cash in full at the beginning of the treatment. The office was soon sold to another orthodontist and was sold again shortly thereafter. When I went for my regular appointment,

I was told I had to see the original doctor at his new office about 45 miles away. I went there and was told that all of the patients were to be treated by the doctor who purchased to practice at the old office. I went back there and was again told I couldn't be treated. I made more calls and visits and learned that the remainder of the aligner trays were at the original office with the doctor who purchased the practice. I went back to the original office and was told again they would not treat me. Finally, I waited until they opened the locked door to allow a patient into the treatment area, I barged through the door went into the doctor's private office and grabbed my aligner trays and hastily left the office. I was phoned and told they called the police. So now it was always kind of a joke that I kept telling my therapist that the police had not been called and that I had not been arrested yet. I had another wonderful doctor who was great. Sometimes he would joke with me. I told him not to mess with me because it wouldn't be the first time a doctor had to call the police on me.

I had now been off of work for three years. Considering my recent bouts of illness, I was unable to be well enough to show up anywhere to work on a regular basis. My employer had sent me a job duty list and asked me to indicate what percent of what jobs I could do. The job duty list did not include the basic work requirement: being able to show up well, on time, on a regular basis. I was still not able to do this.

The few letters I received in response to all the letters I sent, had advised me that in order for me to be approved for long term disability benefits, my workers comp case needed to be accepted (Although this is not what the LTD pamphlet said). The company that processed the long term disability was the same company that held up my workers comp case. That company, in processing my Workers Comp case, ultimately had ten doctors reports and three agreed medical examiner reports indicating I was disabled with a work related illness. In spite of not having approved my case for years, they then agreed the day before the court date that my illness was work related and approved the workers comp case. Once I had the Judge's signature on the worker's comp court papers, I immediately notified LTD and asked them to re-open my case as I was previously advised by letter to do. They sent me a new application to fill out along with a lot of forms not previously required with my first application. I filled them all out. Then they said they needed more paperwork and copies of my medical records (which I had previously already sent them). I was livid. I re-sent the whole box of all my medical records. I filed more fraud complaints and sent a letter to the union. (I was unable to have the union help with my workers comp case because I had an attorney but I was unrepresented for LTD so I could involve the union on this). My letter summarized the information and timeline as follows:

LTD Claim

Request for LTD Benefits - I applied for LTD benefits in January of 2103 and October of 2014. I would like to be approved for the LTD benefits that I am entitled to. To date, three agreed medical examiners and ten doctors have written reports indicating my condition is work related. My Worker's Comp case was accepted by the Court and signed by the judge on October 7, 2014 and I promptly notified the administrator but my LTD benefits have not been approved yet and they have not responded to my recent calls and faxes.

The administrator has not complied with contract deadlines. They have been non responsive and the requirements are not consistent with the government legal Code and third party contract. The following documents the chronology of my application process and non- compliance with requirements.

Initial Application - I filed for long term disability benefits on January 1, 2013. I provided two physician certificates indicating my condition was work related and that I was totally disabled along with concurring reports from five other doctors. I was told that a Worker's

Comp Agreed Medical Examiner (AME) needed to determine if my condition was work related.

5/13/2013 Worker's Comp AME determines condition is work related - On May 13, 2013 the AME issued a report that I was totally disabled with an industrial injury. On June 3, 2013, I sent a letter to the administrator advising them of the AME's findings and requesting my LTD benefits. On August 21 2013, the employer sent a letter indicating that acceptance of the Worker's Comp Case (that was supposed to be accepted within 60 days after the May 13, 2013 AME report, but wasn't) was now suddenly required prior to LTD approval. The governing legal code and the 2012 LTD brochure do not indicate this is a requirement. (The updated LTD brochure for 2013-2014 added this requirement although it is not in the governing legal Code).

8/21/2013 Worker's Comp Administrator Letter says case is accepted - On August 21, 2013, a letter was sent by the administrator indicating my Worker's Comp case was accepted and that I had an industrial injury. I sent many letters inquiring why, after this letter was issued, my LTD benefits were still not approved. On March 12, 2014 I finally got a letter indicating they would re-open my LTD case after the Worker's Comp case was accepted by the Court.

10/7/2014 Worker's Comp Case accepted by the Court and signed by the Judge - On October 7, 2014, the Worker's Comp judge signed the order accepting my case. On October 8, 2014, I sent a letter asking the administrator to re-open the LTD application along with five physician statements (only one was required), medical records and copies of previously submitted application documents. Even though I had previously submitted a complete application, on October 30, 2014, the administrator requested more documents to be provided, many of which are not required as part of a regular LTD application. I provided the documents on 11/11/2014. Then, the on-line update indicated they were "waiting for information from the physician". I called them right way and asked what they were waiting for. They said they needed some AME reports and some other records, all of which they should have already had. In response, on 11/26/2014 I sent them a complete package of all medical records from all doctors. Now, the online update says they are waiting for information from the employer.

Today, January 12, 2015 is over two years from my initial submittal and three years from my date of illness. – It is over three months from my request to re-open the case on October 9, 2014. It is two months since I submitted the additional information they requested on November 11, 2014. It is 47 days since I mailed additional copies of medical records that they already had.

The administrator has not complied with Contract requirements – The Contract states that the administrator shall fully perform, complete and deliver on time, all tasks, deliverables and services.

1. **Seven day deadline not met** – Section 3.1 of Appendix B of the contract states that "the administrator has **seven calendar days** to send the application packet."
    a. I notified the administrator on 10/9/2014 that the judge accepted the workers comp case and asked them to re-open my case per

their letter. The packet that was sent was dated October 30th, **twentyone days** after my letter.

b. The administrator's LTD letter indicates the material is sent to employees who are absent from work for **four months** or longer. My initial absence commenced on 1/30/2012. I did not receive LTD information until **eleven months** later on December 20, 2012.

2. **IME Evaluation never arranged** – Section 3.6 of Appendix B states that if there is a question of causation for employees who have less than five years of service, the administrator shall arrange for an evaluation by an Independent Medical Examiner. This has not happened. I had three AME reports for my workers comp case who all agreed my condition was work related but The LTD administrators have not used these records to accept my case and have NOT scheduled an IME.

3. **Five/Ten day deadline not met during the first and second application process** - Section 3.8 of Appendix B of the Contract states that there will be communication of approval within **(5) working days** of complete claim information and there will be communication of **claim denial within (10) calendar days** of complete claim information. I submitted all requested documents on 11/11/2014 so my application should have been complete on that date. I was told they wanted more records from the doctors (which they already should have had) and then although it is not an application requirement, I submitted a box of complete records on 11/26/2014. I have not heard anything since and my calls have not been answered. As of today, the administrator's website says that they are waiting

for information from my employer. They have not answered what information they are waiting for.

4. **The administrator has established a requirement that is not in the Governing Code or their contract** – The administrator's letters indicate that they require the Worker's Comp case to be accepted prior to an employee with less than five years of service to be eligible. The governing legal code and administrator's contract do not say this.

5. **Even after the worker's comp AME indicated that the condition was work related and after a worker's comp acceptance letter was issued and after the Worker's Comp Case was accepted by the judge, the LTD case has still not been accepted.** – The Governing Legal Code indicates "written proof" of the "extent of the disability" is to be provided. Appendix B of the administrator's contract authorized pursuant to the legal code defines disability. The contract indicates and IME appointment is to be scheduled if there is a question of causation. Nowhere in any of these documents does it indicate a disability can only be validated after acceptance by the third party administrator OR the Worker's Compensation Board. The brochure from 2012 indicates that an employee is eligible for Long Term Disability (LTD) Benefits if they are "disabled as a direct result of an on the job injury or illness." After my complaints, the LTD brochure was amended to state the definition of disability requires the employee to "be disabled as a result of an accepted Worker's Compensation injury." This requirement is not in the governing legal code or administraor's contract. From January 2014 the administrator was processing my workers comp claim and caused the delays in the

acceptance of my worker's comp case until it was accepted on the court date in Oct of 2014.

I applied for LTD benefits in January of 2103, and as I was directed. I requested the re-opening of my case and resubmitted all previous application documents in October 2014 after the judge signed the WC order. Then I reapplied in November 2014 as I was directed. I requested to be approved for the LTD benefits that I was entitled to.

Magically within two days I got a call from the LTD administrator indicating they would be issuing payments within a few days. However, when I got the payment, it was only for a year and a half and at the same time I received an LTD termination letter along with the explanation of benefits. Now, they were saying that for the first part of LTD, the Worker's Comp case had to be accepted to be eligible for benefits. And, that in order for LTD benefits after that, social security must find the employee disabled.

Apparently, this self insured government agency had created rules that were different from the usual State Disability rules. Instead of the usual two years of benefits, they had a shorter benefit window and had additional requirements for the extended benefits.

The following is a summary of issues from my response letter complaining about the fact that the benefits were wrongfully terminated.

I believe the wrongful termination of my LTD benefits can be considered as Bad faith or Fraud based on the legal definitions below.

FRAUD – CA Insurance Code Section 1871.4:

1) It is unlawful to make a knowingly false or fraudulent material representation for the purpose of denying any compensation.
2) It is unlawful to cause to be presented a knowingly false or fraudulent written material statement in opposition to a claim for compensation.

BAD FAITH:

1) Wrongful Denial of Claim and Unreasonable delay in paying benefits
2) Failure to keep the insured informed of significant developments

The reasons for the termination are inconsistent and not legitimate. The administrator has not complied with Contract requirements.

There were four different reasons given for termination of LTD benefits:

1) The on line printout states that "Your claim has been terminated as you are able to perform duties of occupations other than your own."
2) The Check stub says "Status: SUSPENDED"
3) The Acceptance Letter I received on 2/5/2015 indicates that "After this 24-month period, the LTD benefit ceases unless your condition meets the Federal Social Security Act's criteria of total disability."
4) The administrator's second letter I received on 2/5/2015 states "Your failure to submit approval for Medicare benefits has resulted in your claim being terminated effective July 30, 2014."

I do not believe any of the reasons for termination of LTD benefits are valid for the following reasons:

1) The administrators Letter states the LTD benefit ceases unless your condition meets the Federal Social Security Act's criteria of total disability, and defines the Federal Social Security Act's criteria of total disability:

Social Security criteria states that in order for an individual to be considered disabled, he/she must be unable to perform any substantial gainful work due to a medical condition, which has lasted or is expected to last at least twelve (12) months or end in death. The condition must be severe enough to keep a person from working not only in his or her usual job, but also in other substantial gainful work, which is defined as earnings of $1070.00 per month in 2014. Social Security takes into consideration the person's age, education, training, and work experience when a decision is made as to whether he/she can work. Social Security does not consider only whether the individual is able to go back to their old job, or whether or not the individual is able to be hired.

The medical certifications submitted to the administrator by Certified mail in November/December of 2014 state verbatim by three of my doctors that I meet the FSSA criteria for total disability. My medical certifications prove I meet the FSSA requirements, therefore my benefits should not cease. **If these certifications were sufficient in January of 2015 to determine retroactive eligibility for LTD benefits through July 2014, how are they not sufficient for the LTD to continue past the first 24 months after July 2014?**

Excerpts of those medical records certifying the disability are quoted as follows:

1) "The patient is permanently and substantially incapacitated." "The patient meets the requirements of total and permanent disability

under the SSA." "The patient cannot engage in any substantial gainful activity due to the medical impairments listed."

2) "The patient is not able to sustain any gainful activity or employment because…" "The patient meets the requirements of total and permanent disability under the SSA guidelines... If the infection becomes systemic or invasive it can be fatal."

3) "The patient is permanently and totally disabled and cannot engage in any substantial gainful activity because…" "The condition has lasted continuously for two years and can be expected to last continuously for more than 12 months." "The condition must be carefully managed and kept under control. If the condition becomes systemic or invasive it can be fatal."

4) "The patient meets the requirements of total and permanent disability under the SSA." "If the condition becomes systemic or invasive it can be fatal."

5) The administrator's contract Appendix B section 5.12 states that "The final decision for total disability will be determined after 23 months and prior to the end of 24 months." I did not receive the letter with the administrator's position on this decision until three years after my disability claim began.

2) The administrator's letter stated "Your failure to submit approval for Medicare benefits has resulted in your claim being terminated effective July 30, 2014." This does not appear to be a valid reason for denying benefits for the following reasons:

a. The LTD brochure does not mention anywhere that it is a requirement to apply for Medicare in order for LTD benefits to continue. The brochure lists a number of reasons for termination of benefits and not applying for Medicare isn't one of them.

b. The governing legal Code does not mention anywhere that it is a requirement to apply for Medicare in order for LTD benefits to continue.

c. The administrator's Letter dated 2/3/205 accepting my LTD claim does not mention any requirements to apply for Medicare in order for LTD benefits to continue.

d. The administrator's Contract approved by the Governing Board on November 5, 2014 does not mention applying for Medicare.

e. The administrator's Contract Section 3.8 requires the administrator to "State the reason for any claim denial and reference the appropriate Governing Legal Code Section." Where is the reference to a Code Section that requires application for Medicare? There is no reference and there is no code section.

f. The employer's Insurance premium statement indicates that the employee must maintain their company medical coverage in order to be eligible for LTD benefits. Why does this statement say the employee MUST maintain Company insurance but the administrator's letter says the employee MUST apply for Medicare.

g. The LTD brochure states that I am required to continue making health insurance payments while I am in a 'no pay' status.

This means I was required to make Company Insurance payments up until January 2015 when I got the LTD payments and now I am back in a 'no pay' status. Now my coverage is being denied because I didn't apply for Medicare because I was making the required insurance premium payments and covered by the Company group Insurance.

h. Applying for Medicare would reduce the level of coverage for my industrial illness treatments. It is hard enough to get coverage from my company group insurance.

i. In October of 2014 during the open enrollment period, I sent letters and made calls expressing concern because my COBRA was due to expire in a few months. No one told me to apply for Medicare. Instead, The Company put me on the payroll for the month of October so I would be re-enrolled in the health care plan I already had.

j. The Governing Legal Code states: The Company shall furnish the claimant with the appropriate forms for applying for benefits and for filing for proof a disability." I was never notified of any requirement to apply for Medicare. I was never provided with any forms to apply for Medicare. I do not believe it is a legitimate requirement and it deprives me of the right to continue with the insurance I had at the time I became disabled. I need this top of the line insurance to provide the coverage for my rare and unusual illness caused by my employment.

I also had not received the medical expense reimbursements from the Worker's Comp Claim. The Court ordered payments were due November 6th, 2014. A Petition for Penalties had been filed with the Court in addition to the previously filed Serious and Willful Misconduct Petition that was approved by the Worker's Comp court.

So to summarize, I was trying to hit a moving target. New requirements, unsupported by the rules or the law, kept being required at each step of the process.

One of the requirements to be eligible for LTD was to apply for disability retirement with the Company's retirement administration company since the Company does not pay into social security. I had applied a year ago for the Company disability retirement and now oddly enough after I filed all these complaints, I was scheduled to see the retirement company's Independent Medical Examiner (IME). I brought my oxygen and breathed it through a nasal cannula as I now did whenever I had to go into a building where I was not familiar with the level of indoor air quality. I was desperate to avoid any situation that brought on the onset of GTW (Global Thermonuclear War). I never got any re-infections or inflammatory reactions from buildings while using the oxygen.

As part of the exam, they needed to draw blood. To the dismay of myself and the phlebotomist, they could not get any blood to come out in the blood draw. This had been a routine problem as I was usually very dehydrated. Having the blood in the urine and UTI's always made me pee out fluids faster than I could drink it. I had to go back the next day for another try at the blood draw. The person preparing the report called me and asked me some questions. She indicated the reports would say I was unable to perform any of my regular job duties.

I also had some re-testing suggested by my regular toxicologist. Previous blood tests had come up with about 40 things that were abnormal or out of range. There are some blood tests she called "Inflammatory Markers" and we wanted to see how these were doing. One of the tests is C4a. It should be less than 2830. Previously mine was 22,416 but now it was down to 13,262. Another test was TGFB-1 which should be less than 2382. Mine was previously 11,360 but was now down to 7700. I was doing better but still not that great.

Another thing now being required for someone to obtain LTD benefits is for them to submit a disability filing with Social Security and to be deemed disabled by the Social Security office.

Originally the requirement was only to have submitted the application but the Company revised this to mean that the application had to be approved by Social Security for Medicare Part A.

The Company does not pay into social security like 99% of the rest of the citizens of the United States. They have their own retirement plan. However, in order for an employee to be eligible for Long Term Disability, they require the employee to be found disabled by Social Security. And not only must the employee be unable to perform their previous job, they must be deemed unable to perform ANY job in the work force. My main problem with being able to work is that I was sick with flu-like illnesses about half the time. I had sudden onset illnesses that made me sick for weeks at a time. I was constantly on antibiotics. I regularly had many doctor's appointments every week. Two weeks I had seven appointments within the week and in one eight day period, I had eleven appointments, five of which were daily antibiotic injections. What employer would hire me if I called in sick more than half the time?

Under this Medicare Part A program, the employee is not eligible for monetary social security disability, but must process a claim through Social Security to obtain a finding of disability to obtain benefits for Part A Medicare hospitalization only. A process which most of the Social Security Employees are entirely unfamiliar with. The employee is also not able to obtain an attorney to help with this process because, by law, the attorneys can only be paid through a percentage of the monetary benefit the employee would get if found disabled and eligible for monetary social security benefits. And since the monetary benefit for this Company's employees through social security is zero, the attorney cannot collect any fees and therefore will not represent the employee.

So at this point in time, I had an open Worker's Comp Case, a civil Lawsuit against the building owner, I had a Long Term disability

Claim and I was processing a disability retirement claim. Now I was also processing a claim for Part A Medicare through social security by myself, without an attorney.

There was a mediation in the Civil case. I was offered a decent sum of money which my attorney and I declined as it would have hardly covered my massive amount of medical expenses. We opted to continue on with litigation and a jury trial. The day after the mediation, my employer's company filed a lien. They alleged that they should be reimbursed from the civil lawsuit for any money they paid me from worker's comp. I was glad I had not accepted the offer because they would have made a claim against it and I would have ended up with nothing. So for the next year, we would be preparing for trial.

For the next several years, in addition to seeing my treating doctors, the opposing counsels for my various legal battles would send me to their independent medical experts.

One of the first experts I was sent to during this period was a psychiatrist for the defense in my Civil lawsuit. Before the date of my appointment, I went to the building to anticipate if I might possibly potentially have any adverse reaction to the air quality in the building. I did a walk though of the building and by the back stairwell of the third floor (where the psychiatrists office was) I heard a buzzing alarm coming from the stairwell. The alarm was coming from the HVAC system indicating that the air filter needed to be changed, the cover over the HVAC system was missing and the stairwell was filthy. I called my attorney and told him my displeasure about having to be required to spend eight hours being examined in a place where I could potentially have an allergic reaction. I also called the building management and made a complaint. I was told I was required by law to go to the appointment so I used my portable oxygen and had someone drive me there.

The night before the appointment I was not well and started peeing blood, something that now happened frequently. I was awake most of the night and I was first in line as I waited outside the urgent care before it opened at 8:00 am. I took a photo of my blood red urine sample and I saw the doctor. I got a copy of the urine test result, got my medication and made it to the psychiatrist in time for the 10:00 am appointment.

The psychiatrist was incredulous and after a conversation with my attorney, he decided this was a stressor that could affect the results of the tests so they opted to postpone it.

In the mean time, Social Security had already denied my application several times at several different levels which I understand is standard operating procedure. They were now directing me to see one of their doctors prior to an administrative hearing. Having gotten nose bleed allergic reactions and illnesses from several medical facilities, I just began to always use the bottled oxygen as it was the only thing I had found that would keep me from getting a nose bleed in a building where I would always get one if I didn't use the oxygen. It just so happened that I had a fall and injured my leg and arthritic knee prior to the doctor appointment and it was difficult to manage crutches and the oxygen tank. I had a friend drive me to the appointment and I went in a wheel chair with my swollen leg propped up.

I had a second appointment with the Civil lawsuit psychiatrist selected by opposing counsel. I used oxygen as was my standard protocol and I had a friend drop me off. I realized I had forgot reading glasses and he agreed to go to the store and get some.

Prior to the appointment, I had been having episodes of very low blood pressure. The lowest I had was 79/47. When my blood pressure was that low, it was like I was going to pass out but I never did. I would lay on the couch at home contemplating whether to call for paramedics. I would usually drink water, eat salty foods and kept moving my arms and legs to try to keep from passing out and to keep the blood flowing.

This day, when I got to the psychiatrist office for my agreed medical exam, I was feeling especially unwell and I was worried about my blood pressure being low. I asked the doctor if he had a blood pressure cuff which he didn't. I asked if I could answer his questions while I was laying on the couch. He continued with his routine questions but then became concerned and pulled up a screen on his computer and started asking me questions if I was having chest pain, if I was sweating etc. He then called for the paramedics and I was taken to the Emergency Room. When my friend came back with the glasses, he was told the HIPPAA laws prevented them from telling him where I was. The receptionist confided in my friend that the Doctor was an asshole and that I had been taken to a nearby emergency room.

The third time I had an appointment scheduled with this doctor, my son had passed away the week before. Once again, they chose to not evaluate me at the time and indicated the appointment should be re-scheduled. It took months and years for the additional Medical Examiner appointments for this doctor and LACERA and Social Security to get scheduled.

MY SON

In the mean time, I had to deal with the grief over the loss of my son Bobby. He was 27 years old and 6'-10" when he passed away.

He had the opportunity in life to do many things a lot of people would not usually get to do. One of his childhood friends took him to the TV Kid's Choice Awards, a closed movie industry event by invitation only. Another friend took him to the Long Beach Grand Prix. His elementary school had go karts there during the summer and they got to drive the go karts. He got to be a body double for a famous NBA player in a commercial for a bank.

Bobby on set at the filming of the commercial with fake hair and beard to look like NBA player

His father Gerry's family lived in Belgium and during trips back to Belgium to see his grandmother, we took trips to Rome, Paris, Prague etc. In Belgium they take vacations during the winter and we went skiing in Austria on "winter sport" with Gerry's family.

When Bobby was in high school, we couldn't afford to buy him a car but his uncle gave us a non-working old Crown Victoria with the police package named "Big Blue". Bobby spent his lunch hours in high school auto shop replacing the entire engine and transmission and got the car to run. I went to his high school every day on my lunch hour to deliver him two, foot long deli sandwiches for lunch. The lunch lines were too long form him to be able to get any food during the allotted lunch hour. By the time he almost got to the front of the line to order food, it was already time to go back to class. His car had a push button entry code and I would use the code to open the car door and leave the sandwiches in the car for him to retrieve.

There are two things that are sacred to "seven footers" (guys that are close to 7'-0" tall): FOOD and SLEEP. They need LOTS of both. My brother also has two tall sons who are 6'-7" and we share stories and photos of the meals they eat. One of my favorite photos was my son having dinner using a pizza pan for a plate. It was covered with hamburgers, hot dogs and pizza slices that he ate. My favorite food story of my nephews is when he took an entire box of Costco taquitos and carefully arranged them like a log house pyramid on a plate, microwaved it and then proceeded to eat the entire stack of taquitos.

Bobby's dad bought him a new Toyota Tacoma truck when he went off to college. He was on the college basketball team and as an athlete, got priority registration status. While he was only on the team for one year, the priority athlete status lasted all four years. This priority registration helped him immensely as he was able to easily apply for and be registered for the classes he needed.

He liked to fly remote control helicopters, airplanes and drones and suckered me into paying for an endless supply of parts and new flying machines when the old ones crashed. He had one tiny drone with flashing lights that he could easily fly around inside our house with our high ceilings. He laughed as he would fly it around and chase the cat and the dog or buzz it by people who were sitting in the chairs.

In college, he met someone who I will refer to as the "Black Widow". I later learned the way she met him was to intentionally steal his phone and then call me (identified in the phone as Mom) saying she had found the phone and asked me to have him call her to get his phone back.

She went with us on family vacations including trips to Rome and Holland and spent many weekends staying with my son at our spacious home in a nice subdivision in a planned community. Her parents, grandparents, aunts, sister and brother-in-law all lived within a half mile radius of each other. Bobby always referred to this area of Los Angeles where her family lived as "The Hood" and complained of hearing gun shots in the evenings in the area.

When they graduated from college, she refused to move to our area of town or in the outskirt suburban communities with in-expensive housing and more job opportunities for my son. When they were looking for a property to buy, she turned her nose at everything except a property in her parent's neighborhood. I had no idea how close it was to her parent's house until they came walking by his new house while they were out on their neighborhood walk while we were helping my son to move-in. The black widow convinced him to get a job near where her family lived. The job was in the same office complex where she worked and they car-pooled to work together.

Her family would go camping every year on vacation. Bobby complained about not liking the camping trips because he didn't like being the "Sherpa". It is also kind of miserable for a guy that is 7'-0" tall to be crammed in a tiny sleeping bag in a small tent. He also wasn't fond of being around her bossy mother and sister. He said her mom would get on a tear and in a shrieking voice would bark out orders to everyone. He just wasn't in to being bossed around.

One day my son called me in a panic. The Black Widow was all bent out of shape because he had not yet proposed and so at his request, I threw together an impromptu proposal party at our house and he proposed to her. Then she went on about planning the wedding. Our community has a lovely clubhouse overlooking a lake. I offered to pay for the venue and make the arrangements for the venue for them to have the wedding there.

Three months after the wedding, it was time for the black widow's annual family camping trip. My son was busy spending long hours at work earning his biggest commissions ever and got himself out of having to go on the trip. Two weeks after the camping trip, the Black Widow inexplicably moved her things out of the house while he was at work. WTF?

Who does that? She bullied him into buying property and moving near her family in a sketchy neighborhood, bullied him into proposing, getting married, getting a job near the house and now she inexplicably accuses him of cheating and moves out while he is at work?

How could he possibly be cheating? They carpool to work together and he was home every night and they were together at my house on weekends. He had been working long hours and was making his biggest commissions ever.

My son was incredibly despondent. He was trying to understand what happened. The only thing we could figure out was that he was being punished for not going on the camping trip. My son scheduled and attended counseling sessions for him and the black widow. I'm told that when the guy volunteers for and attends counseling sessions, he is not the one that's cheating. One of his friends, a mental health professional, suggested to me that she and/or members of her family were narcissistic sociopaths.

Kevin stayed with us one weekend and on Saturday night, we had dinner at his favorite restaurant, Chili's, with a group of his friends. He went back to his house the next night, Sunday evening that weekend. By Monday morning he was dead.

He made a suicide post on Facebook and put alerts on the post so that my daughter and the Black Widow would see the alert immediately. My daughter tried to call him but it went to voice mail. My daughter called us and I hopped in the car to drive there while my husband tried to call him on the phone.

My husband eventually got ahold of the black widow who said she had been talking to our son on the phone and that her new room mate had called the police. She said she thought he was OK because she heard the police come and say something like: "suspect in custody". When I got to the scene, it was obvious he was deceased.

As the first one at his house, I wanted to obtain anything that would be important before the black widow got there. I took his laptop, backpack, file box, unlocked safe and anything else I could find that might be important and loaded it into my truck and locked it. I quickly looked through his file box. When I was helping him move out of our house, we had put this file box together and put his important papers in it. Those papers that we carefully inserted into file folders that we labeled that included his tax returns passport, birth certificate, medical records, etc and A WILL. At that time, I asked him why he had a will and he said that in one of his college insurance estate planning classes they each had to prepare a will, and then they each took turns witnessing and signing each others wills. Now the WILL was NOT in the file box and the safe was empty. His WILL was gone before this happened.

My sister arrived to my son's house from Atlanta, my brother arrived from San Jose and my daughter arrived from San Diego, all before the black widow and her parents made it six blocks from their house to the scene.

My son had changed the locks after the black widow had moved. Now her father, immediately upon entering, set about removing the new locks from the door and taking the old locks (which they had keys to) off the desktop and installing them. The first words out of the black widows mouth were that he didn't have a will. How could she already be claiming there was no will? I knew he had one. After they left, we scoured the house. The will I had personally previously seen was not there. It had already been removed prior to the locks being changed and before his passing.

The day after his death, we got a call from his friend, an insurance agent. Bobby had a life insurance policy and the black widow and her sister had already come by to collect the life insurance but they were not the named beneficiaries. He said we should collect the policy ASAP to prevent them from having any claim to it. The black widow and her sister also showed up that day at his office to inquire about his company life insurance and they told her to go fuck herself.

Later, I ran across an e-mail Bobby had found. Six months prior to his death, the black widow and her sister had obtained an opinion from and her sister's attorney friend who told them that the wife would be the beneficiary of his life insurance policies regardless of the named beneficiary on the policies. They erroneous believed, they would get all of his life insurance money regardless of who the named beneficiaries were. Bobby, having been a life insurance salesman, had a lot of policies on himself that he had purchased to meet his quotas. But pretty much everyone in the family also had numerous insurance policies of some sort or other that we had purchased through him to help him meet his quotas.

At the funeral home, both of our families sat around the table to make the arrangements. The funeral staff indicated that, due to limitations at the County Health Department, they are only able to provide four copies of the death certificate that would be available in a few days and asked how many each of us wanted. Originally it was agreed for each family to have two certificates. But the black widow's mother called her out of the room. When they came back in, they said they need ALL of the copies for insurance purposes and we would get none.

The black widow put on quite a show at the funeral. I did not see it but my brother was appalled as she wailed away and draped herself across the casket.

At the time, LBD's (little black dresses) were in style and I had included LBD's with recent birthday gifts and Christmas presents to various family members. Now, here was my daughter, her friend, my niece, and the black widow, all wearing the LBD's I had bought them. The black widow had selected the big & tall tuxedo suit that I had bought for my son for his wedding, for him to be buried in.

It was a touching memorial service. Everyone had great stories about Kevin. Especially memorable to me was the story about how Kevin was lifting and upgrading his brand new Tacoma that his dad had just bought for him and was taking a chain saw to the roof to open a hole to install a moon roof. Another story was how he and a friend (both who had NOT been drinking) got tired of waiting in a line of cars to go through a DUI checkpoint on the road to our house and tried to go around it which immediately caught the attention of the police who pulled them over. My son put on some flashing glow in the dark light up sunglasses and got out of the truck doing a goofy dance and had the police laughing in stitches. How does that happen? If I did that, I would have been arrested for sure.

The next day I beat a path to the health department myself and got my own copies of the death certificate. I e-mailed the black widow a copy before they got theirs just to let them know I already had my own copies. The certificate said his death was ruled a suicide.

The black widow refused to give us Bobby's company phone that had been purchased and was being paid for by my husband's company, where my son had still been doing work on the weekends. I wanted to look at the phone to see what correspondence she and my son had had prior to his passing but she refused to give us the phone. I purchased a phone exactly like the one he had. I had the phone company block his phone and transfer all possible data to the new phone. I was hoping to see any text messages, photos, phone logs etc.

As soon as I fired the phone up, it started pinging with seven voice mails that had come in. The first voice mail was from my daughter on the night he passed saying she saw his FB post and asked him to answer the phone. The next voice mail was 19 seconds long and at first I heard nothing and then I heard the sound of TWO gunshots several seconds apart and then nothing but some background noise. Next was my husband's call asking him to answer the phone. I have to say, it's chilling to hear a recording of TWO gunshot sounds on the phone of your deceased son who allegedly committed suicide.

I went back and carefully listened to the 19 second phone call. It had two, distinct explosive gun shot sounds. I played it for my nephew who was visiting at the time. I was not able to make it any louder because I couldn't operate the android phone and it wasn't yet set up with any of the apps or settings.

I was in shock. How was there a voice mail on my deceased son's phone with TWO gunshot sounds on it? I spent many hours trying to figure out how this was possible? I discovered by accident when I tried it on my phone, that at that time, if you were on a phone call and tried to do a voice recording with the app, it would record to voice mail.

I went on line and checked the phone records. The black widow was on the phone with him when he passed. The phone call lasted five minutes past the time of death. How could she have heard the police say suspect in custody if he shot himself? How could he have shot himself if he was on the phone? How did she not know he had shot himself if she was on the phone until 5 minutes after the time of death? He did own a gun. It was a .357 magnum. If he shot himself with that, it should have made one heck of a loud BANG. How did she not hear it?

I went to the funeral home and asked questions. Was there one bullet hole or two? They said one bullet hole wound. Detective Joe Kenda on the "Homicide Hunter" TV show episode about an alleged suicide says that a .357 magnum gun shot leaves a hole the size of a microwave. What they told me certainly didn't indicate anything the size of a microwave. The police records indicated the police tried to apply a chest seal at the scene. It would not be possible to apply a chest seal to a hole the size of a microwave.

I looked at the coroner's report. First of all, it did not say what caliber of bullet was taken out. That's odd. The coroner did not take any photos. The report said that a gun shot residue test was done. I asked for the results of the test. I was told the test was taken but never processed. I sent letters asking for them to process it and I got the results. There was ZERO gun shot particles in his gunshot residue test. A regular positive residue test can have 20,000 to 40,000 particles. Well that's odd.

A year later, I got a letter indicating the alleged weapon he shot himself with was no longer needed for evidence and that I could obtain possession of it by filling out some papers and coming in to pick it up. I came by and the alleged suicide weapon was in a box along with the five bullets and an empty casing that had been removed from the six openings of the revolver. They said it had been processed and that all evidentiary value had been removed. I was able to take possession of the gun but they would not let me have the bullets at the same time. I took photos of the bullets and left. I made an appointment to come back later for the bullets. I made many phone calls attempting to have the gun forensically analyzed but no one would do it. I wanted to know: had the gun been fired?, was there high velocity blood spatter on it?, etc.

A friend helped me make an appointment with the coroner. I wanted to see the photos of the bullet wound and of his hands and to inquire on the caliber of the bullet that had been removed. But there were NO coroner photos and there was no information on what kind of bullet was taken out. The only photos they had were the ones taken by the police at the scene. The photos of his hands did not appear to show any blood spatter on the hands. There was a photo of a police officer's hand holding five un-spent bullets in the casings but no empty casing. That's odd. When you eject the bullets from a 357 revolver, you push a button and the cylinder pops to the side and you can dump the bullets out of the revolver. How do you dump the cylinder and have the five bullets fall out but not the empty casing? Shouldn't the photo show five bullets AND an empty casing? Then we asked to see the bullet that had been removed from the body. But we were told that the police had already come by THE DAY BEFORE and obtained it. He said there was a log where they signed it out but we were not able to see the log or to know who signed it out. How did the police know we would be going there inquiring? Well that's odd.

I obtained and looked at the transcripts from the police radio correspondence. One of the officers was named Danny. The transcript said: Danny, got a rifle on him? Answer: Affirmative. Then, "male shot", "male shot". They did not say: he shot himself.

I had to file a lawsuit and issue a subpoena to obtain video taken of the scene. It is dark and grainy and it is difficult to discern anything and definitely had been edited. The only thing that is noticeably NOT visible is a muzzle flash. You would think in the darkness, you would see the muzzle flash from a 357 magnum, but there wasn't one. That's odd.

A lot of people see me as a grieving mother who can't accept the fact that her son shot himself, but there are a lot of things that just don't add up.

I was discussing these oddities and the actions of the black widows family with my sons friend who was a mental health therapist. She said that the actions of the family were the actions of sociopaths and narcissists. I met with my son's boss to obtain his personal effects and she used the same words: narcissist and sociopath.

WHAT IS A NARCISSIST
OR SOCIOPATH?

I did not really understand what a narcissist or sociopath was. I started doing some research. My sister and I found information on the internet and shared it with each other. We began to realize our mother, who I always believed had some mental health issues was a Narcissistic Sociopath. Here we were in our 50's and how had we not yet figured out that our mother was a Narcissitic Sociopath. We started to compile information on spotting and understanding narcissistic/sociopathic behavior and it all fitted her to a tee. It was if they were describing her! We also saw articles about ACON's: Adult Children of Narcissitic Parents and realized this was who we were.

I put together a booklet of the articles for my sister and called it "Narcissitic Personality disorder for Dummies". It included the following Quick Reference Guide:

NARCISSISTIC PERSONALITY DISORDER

QUICK REFERENCE GUIDE

11 signs you or someone you know might be a narcissist

1. Dominating the conversation/need to be the center of attention/ need for everything to be about them
2. Not listening, only waiting for their turn to talk again

3. Thinking everyone else is stupid, need to tell them what to do
4. Rules weren't made for them, they break the rules and love it
5. They find justification (people's mistakes) for being mean to those people
6. They manipulate/bully people to get what they want
7. They have an exaggerated sense of entitlement
8. They must win at everything, are terrible at losing, blame everyone else
9. They feel like no one ever appreciates them enough
10. They hate waiting and feed off of instant gratification
11. Can't commit to serious relationship

6 things a narcissist might say to manipulate you

1. "Nobody else feels that way, you're the only person I have these issues with" "You're remembering that wrong, It didn't happen that way"
2. "You're so .. self-centered/paranoid/controlling ..."
3. "Non-compliments - off handed insults"
4. "Come on, you know I didn't mean it that way,
5. You're just too sensitive"
6. "They don't understand our relationship. They just never felt love that strong"

11 sentences narcissists & sociopaths say to manipulate you

1. I hate drama... You're just being dramatic
2. You' re... crazy ... irresponsible ... bi-polar...jealous ...
3. You're ... too sensitive .... To all of their insults and bad behavior
4. You misunderstood
5. You can't live without me
6. You don't appreciate anything I do
7. Well you waited to the last minute to get this organized
8. I didn't know I was the one to choose the restaurant.
9. I didn't know we were going to make arrangements by e-mail

10. Is that the best outfit you could come up with?
11. Well couldn't you at least have ….

9 comebacks for dealing with a Narcissist

1. "No"
2. "Stay on topic and don't change the subject"
3. "I will believe it when I see it."
4. I'm not overly emotional. I am assertive, strong-willed and impassioned
5. "I have learned from and moved on from my mistakes"
6. "I refuse to be afraid."
7. "Slow down there speedy"
8. "I am not the bad guy here"
9. The world does not revolve around you"

Endless amount of nasty tools used by narcissists. These include:

Outrageous lies/bullying in order to gain whatever goal the narcissist has in mind.

Gas-lighting techniques in order to get you to doubt yourself.

Imagined allies to back up his or her claims.

Malicious comments to maim you.

Attacks on your integrity to disarm you.

Expert projection to make what he or she did your fault.

Purposeful outrageous and childish non-sensical comments to incense you.

Refusal to remain on the topic at hand.

Insistence on boundaries within the conversation, granting him or her all the rights to continue speaking, and you none.

Discard and abandonment techniques regardless of the state you are in. (The more distressed you are the more delight in abandoning you).

Attacking you in regard to your distress, hysteria or anger that has occurred within the argument, constantly reminding you of the outburst you had in response to their outrageous behavior.

The ability to use any of the above (plus more) to purposefully punish you, and create the highest level of anguish possible.

We shared this information with our older brother. Having studied the narcissistic personality traits, my sister and I closely observed my mother when we were at a restaurant ordering lunch while visiting her. We were amazed how everything she said or did was text book narcissistic personality traits. Later, when our father passed away and we had to attend his funeral and be in the presence of our mother, I anticipated the comments she would make and created our own quick reference guide to be able to deal with her.

QUICK REFERENCE GUIDE – RESPONSES TO A NARCISSIST

I don't appreciate …being insulted… malicious comments .. contradictory statements …being accused of… being antagonized

I don't appreciate being blamed. People hate being blamed.

Just acknowledge something needs to be fixed and fix it.

It's upsetting to me to … hear that… to be accused of… to be …..

I'm not happy with comments intended to… insult me…

I feel like I'm being bossed around…I think I'm smart enough to know what to do..

Why would you even bring up something like that? Then change the subject

Why are we discussing that? We are here to celebrate your birthday

Well why is that a topic of discussion? We are here to celebrate your birthday..

When _____, I feel _____,

When I hear that, I feel… offended… insulted…

I don't appreciate having my feelings misrepresented

I'm very disappointed… to hear that ….

Sounds like…. I'm being insulted…. I don't deserve to be insulted

Sounds like ….I'm being blamed for something I had no responsibility for…

Sounds like …. the subject is being changed

I don't appreciate….. being accused of something I had nothing to do with I don't have the time or the crayons to explain this to you

Why is the subject being changed? Why am I being insulted? I am hurt!

Why am I being bossed around? I'm capable of making good decisions

Why are those statements so confusing? Can't those statements be more clear?

I feel like that statement is only to try to upset me… anger me… antagonize me…

You must think I'm stupid that you tell me what to do all the time

I didn't travel all the way from California to have my hairstyle insulted.

I'm not… overly emotional… I'm assertive, strong willed and impassioned

I don't appreciate intimidating comments intended to …bully me… make me agree to something

I don't appreciate continually being told …conflicting statements … obvious lies

I don't appreciate being accused of being… too sensitive…jealous… bitter…

You are just projecting.

I don't appreciate being singled out. I'm sure everyone else feels that way.

I'm not buying into the poor me act. Stay on topic and don't change the subject.

I refuse to be... afraid.... Intimidated... insulted

I am not the bad guy here

Slow down there speedy

I will believe it when I see it

I have learned from and moved on from my mistakes

I realized that some of the people I worked with over the years were serious Narcissistic Sociopaths. The horrible supervisor who destroyed the lives and careers of those who she supervised had seriously extreme sociopathic traits.

And now, here were sociopathic, Narcissistic people that had destroyed my son's life. I found a shocking e-mail the black widow's sister had written to her and her mother. If there are any questions about the normalcy of the family, the text of the evil ranting e-mail is as follows:

I cannot meet with him, ever, because we will likely have to call the police. I want to kick in the balls so hard he can never use his parts again... I want to stab his eyes out. He is the kind of man who deserves to rot in a cell. His empty wind of hot air fuels my hate fire. He is the mold in the bottom of the sewer line and the putrid smell that plagues it is his sense of right and wrong. The vile vomit that erupts at the thought of him will drown him in acid burning his flesh. I imagine his face in the curb with the weight of the world slamming his head into the concrete. But I ride on the back of the beast screaming at the top of my lungs. My voice will make his ears bleed and he will hear the roar of my fight. The fury in my eyes will burn his soul. His tears will fill a bloody river and flow through the desolation that once was his heart. He will taste the salty blood that once was his honor as it pours out of him and his chest will cave under the pressure of his guilt. My fists are ferocious and with my words fly daggers. I will sweep the leg of the convictions he stands on. His head will spin for I will surround his thoughts and he will fear the darkness that follows him. The clash of thunder looming over his head is the sound of my vengeance raking across his face. With the wrath of the dragon's fire, I will burn his core. And from the ashes I will fly with the wings of the phoenix. He will catch no breath, no reprieve, for once I am done with him, my King will crash down on him with the lightning and thunder of an almighty

God. He dug his own grave on this one. With the bite of a great white and strength and anger of a boar, he has messed with the bull and now he will get the horns and they're going up his ass!

Who writes stuff like that to their sister about her husband?

I never did figure out how there could be a recording of two gun shots sounds on his phone, no blood or gun shot residue on his hands, and no muzzle flash other than the probability that someone else had shot him and fired twice because the first shot missed. I did my best to obtain as much information as I could but there was nothing definitive.

It is very special to have a child who is 6'-10" (a seven footer) and I compiled some information about what it is like.

HOW TO FEED AND CARE FOR YOUR SEVEN FOOTER

This chapter was originally intended for Basketball coaches that sought out tall players but were absolutely clueless about the special needs of a seven footer. They routinely had basketball camps with the seven footers scheduled to sleep in 6'-0" long bunk beds that had headboards and footboards. Players would always have to pull the mattress out of the bed and sleep on the mattress on the floor with their feet hanging off the mattress. The coaches never properly planned for the players to have properly scheduled meals. The point guards can thrive on a candy bar and a coke but if a seven footer hasn't had a meal in two or three hours, his stomach starts digesting itself. The coaches always thought that if they whipped the big guys harder they could get more out of them. Not so. They can't run on an empty tank. You just have to feed them large quantities of food at regular intervals and then they are good to go. Some of the coaches knew that the big guys needed up to 10,000 calories a day just to keep from losing weight on practice days. If you have never seen a seven footer preparing themselves some food, it really is a special treat. My favorite image of my 6'-7" nephews typical snack was to take an entire box of taquitos and arrange them on a plate like a log cabin and place the entire structure in the microwave. My son would take a pizza pan and use it for a dinner plate. It would contain, slices of pizza, several hot dogs and several hamburgers.

I grew up in a family of over six footers and the situations in this book were par for the course. For anyone not familiar with these unique problems, this is for you.

An elephants gestation period is 21 months.

As a mom of a seven footer you can plan on your pregnancy taking longer than normal. My family history is pregnancies run at least two weeks longer than normal and the babies are definitely at the large end of the scale.

Regular infant feeding schedules will not apply. They will need solid food in a matter of weeks, not months. When the baby is born, it will want a lot of food and wants it NOW W W W W!

The Doctors will be unable to predict the child's height, the charts don't go that high:

> Basic math: Massive quantities of food in = massive quantities of food out. You have to change a lot of very full diapers.

They can be very competitive, even in pre-school. My son always got the good eater and good napper awards. Then he got an award for having the most good eater and good napper awards.

Other moms with think your 3'-6" tall child is "slow". Why is he still in a diaper, why can't he talk. BECAUSE HE'S ONLY TWO YEARS OLD.

You may become BFF's with the local orthopedic doctor. Quickly growing bones seem to break more easily. My seven footer had seven broken bones. Here is my daughter (who grew to be 6'-1) and her cousin (who grew to be 6'-4) in a photo with matching arm casts.

The other sports teams always tried to disqualify your team for using an older kid (my son on the far left) so you always have to have his birth certificate handy at games.

I admit, I am guilty of this too. My daughter played against a team with the sister of an NBA player on it and her mom had to show me the birth certificate for me to believe her daughter, that was the same age as mine, was that much taller than mine.

You always end up paying adult fares at the movies and the train station. As a child, my father always had to pay adult fare on the Chicago street cars because they would not believe he was only ten. But they never had to worry about anyone picking on them on the bus.

Its always a challenge getting enough long beds. We went on a family trip to Italy and we had: My son 6'-10, my husband and his friend both 6'-6", my sister and two brothers all 6'-5, me 6'-3" and my daughter 6'-1". We finally found a Villa with 6 king size beds. This was not an easy task in Europe and Italy.

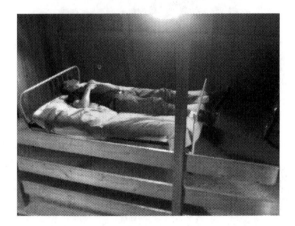

We did not have a problem spotting our son at graduation. The usher came to reprimand him for standing on the chair during the ceremony but quickly walked away embarrassed when he realized my son was standing on the ground.

As a tall woman, I always get glared at with looks like: why the heck are you wearing high heels, aren't you tall enough, only to see them look down and realize with an embarrassed look on their face that I'm wearing flip flops.

There are two things that are sacred to a big man....

1) FOOD....

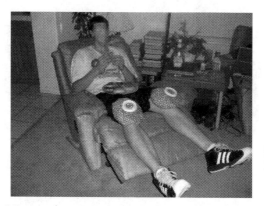

Notice the pizza pan, used as a plate, full of hamburgers taken after basketball practice.

One night I stopped at a local fast food place and picked up the family meal for seven for our family of four. My son ate the whole thing. The photo below was a snack before dinner one night: four slices of pizza and two hamburgers.

Here's a Safety tip: Never try to take food away from a seven footer. AND the second thing sacred to a seven footer:....

2) Sleep

Here's another safety tip: Do not try to wake a sleeping giant. If you absolutely must wake them, wave some aromatic food in front of their face.

A doctor once told us that growth only happens during sleep. If you want your kids to be tall, make sure they get enough sleep.

You know you have a seven footer when you get a hand written note from the local grocery store thanking you for your business. We got such a hand written holiday card from the local supermarket when Bobby was in high school.

When you are a seven footer, any breed can be a lap dog.

You might need to make sure you always get FULL SIZE rental cars.

You won't be able to drive a sports car with the top on.

Its not hard to pick out the relatives in the old family photos. My great, great uncle was on the Chicago Fire Department around the time of the great Chicago fire. A photo of his battalion and horse drawn fire engine is on display at the Chicago Fire Museum.

Seven footers are handy for heavy lifting. He didn't like to go camping with friends because he always had to be the Sherpa.

You know you are tall when Big Foot's Foot Prints lead right to your house...

Because they're yours.

The clerks at the main Los Angeles Big & Tall store always welcomed me by name when I walked in the store. It was the only place I could buy off the rack clothes for my seven footer. Any other store branches did not stock those sizes and it had to be ordered.

My son was very patient. When he worked with my husband and met with many different customers, he never tired of people constantly asking him the same pointless questions:

HOW TALL ARE YOU? … WOW YOU'RE TALL
HOW'S THE WEATHER UP THERE?
DO YOU PLAY BASKETBALL?
ONE OTHER THING ABOUT SEVEN FOOTERS …
TRY NOT TO PISS THEM OFF

Then it was back to the task of dealing with my employer, going to my medical appointments, doing my daily treatment regimen and managing everyday life.

RETALIATION FOR MY DISABILITY COMPLAINT – HIGHER PROPERTY TAX

My husband and I purchased an inexpensive single family fixer upper as a rental property and paid all cash (from the inheritance) for it. The job of establishing the taxable value of the property we purchased was with a satellite office of my employer which was the office who was now managing my personnel file. Normally, a property is assessed at the purchase price. However, in a cash sale, the actual price of the property comes into question. The tax valuation office, under the jurisdiction of the government agency where I had been employed, deemed that the value of the property was $40,000 or 24% higher than what we paid for it. With my illness, I was not able to attend the initial Assessment Appeal meeting to question the assigned property value. I hired a friend who was a tax agent to attend the meeting. We went over the facts of the case and he went off to argue the case. When I saw him after the meeting his face was pale and ashen. I asked what happened. His declaration of what happened (attached as an Exhibit to a Lawsuit) is as follows:

DECLARATION OF REGISTERED TAX AGENT

I, declare as follows:

1. I was retained as a registered tax agent to represent some homeowners on a property tax issue concerning their acquisition of a residential property and to attend the first scheduled and requested property tax assessment hearing on May 18, 2016.

2. Upon arrival I attempted to check-in for the hearing on the owner's behalf, wearing my picture ID badge with my name and tax agent number clearly displayed in plain view.

3. A verbal assault towards me began as soon as the hearing manager who was an extremely aggressive, large and loud African American woman, and by other employees as soon as they heard the property owner's name. They said they had been *"waiting for me to arrive"* and appeared to show absolutely no concern of any repercussions from their actions, towards me, claiming they were *"justified"* in doing *"the right thing."*

1

4. The hearing manager stated and informed others at the hearing office that *"My* <u>*wife*</u> *has a disability claim against the Company."*

   The officer further threatened me several times with *"calling the Sherriff"* if I did not do exactly as she *ordered* me to, or to *speak* without receiving *"permission from her first"*

5. The manager further stated that the owner, while incredulously still accusing her of being my *"wife"* even after I *repeatedly* informed her otherwise, *"had a worker's comp claim and that she and I were committing*

workers comp fraud", and further, *"My "wife" and I were committing "property tax fraud"*

6. The owner's husband's actual height is 6'-'6" while the wife's height is 6'-3" and mine, being 5'-3", clearly represented the enormous degree of delusional impairment exhibited by the hearing manager and other employees who stated they *"knew all about me"* and *"were waiting for me* illustrating quite convincingly just how baseless and outrageous their *total lack of percipient truthful knowledge actually was.*

7. Additional statements made by the hearing manager and other employees at the time included; "I should *be ashamed of this deceitful attempt"* apparently referring to my *allegedly being the homeowner* and that both of us, (my alleged wife) and I, *"Had no business asking for a property tax hearing"*! and again falsely claiming and accusing me of being a current Employee.

8. The hearing manager antagonized me by calling me *"Whitey"* and *"No Good Cracker"* and tried to engage me in a fight outside in the parking lot.

9. I was ordered by the hearing manager to *"remain seated"* in the larger room waiting area, before being allowed to transfer to the desk of the scheduled hearing officer, who cancelled the hearing immediately on the orders of the hearing manager for my *"leaving the seating area"* without *"her permission"* after I was instructed to come forward when I heard my case being called.

10. The hearing manager's baseless slander, inflammatory behavior and invective manner provide good cause to *consider* as one reason, the owner's property taxes may have been increased in blatant retaliation for the owner's having a Worker's Comp Claim.

11. One of the most significant factors (and there surely are several) about this *verbal assault* directed upon me

is that it was_premeditated as the additional listed facts and further actions of the assistant and her employees demonstrate:

1) As I stated, the manager accused me and the owner of committing disability fraud and *all three of us,* myself and the owners of property tax fraud.

2) At the end of the incident as I was trying to leave, the manager stated she and her willing co-worker wanted to "kick my ass" and tried to provoke me into a *physical* fight with them on the steps outside building!

3) The manager *repeatedly,* referred to me "whitey" and "no good cracker."

4) Afterwards I spoke to a number of Company personnel following the incident, including the supervisor, which resulted in our hearing being rescheduled after improperly being listed *"as conducted, heard and denied"!*

5) Rightfully concerned for my safety, I requested that all future hearings regarding this property be held at a different location to avoid further contact with any the employees responsible for this disgusting behavior and upon being informed that the hearing manager would continue being *in charge* of the Newhall location!

12. I was informed by the owner's/employee's supervisor, who I immediately spoke to by phone, that the owner/employee had violated some arbitrary "personal rule" of her supervisor (who was now managing her personnel file), and this may have been the cause and catalyst behind the manager's and her fellow employee's outrageous actions. This personal rule was for employees to

touch base with their supervisor if they purchase a property. Although no such rule is written or was ever communicated to the employee.

13. The behavior and conduct at the hearing appointment on May 18th, 2016, especially the manager's, and one of her co-worker's was quite disturbing and extremely uncomfortable and I was not provided the hearing we were assigned and had a *scheduled* appointment for.

14. The Company, incredulously saw no urgency or need to make changes after being informed of the manager's conduct, or her co-worker's despite the allegations being promptly and independently reported and substantiated.

The most significant factor about this ambush of my tax agent is that is was premeditated. As soon as they heard my last name, the attack began. They said they had been waiting for us. The tax agent was told the supervisor in charge of overseeing my personnel file advised them to do this.

We were denied our hearing. I was denied an informal review. I received a letter regarding this situation we complained to the supervisors about. The gave me five days to respond, but the letter was dated six days before I got it. The response deadline had already expired. The letter indicated they had been attempting to contact me but no such numbers or calls were in my phone logs. A mediation was then scheduled to resolve this issue. After I submitted a mediation brief in advance of the meeting, it was cancelled without investigation or due process. My tax agent was persistent and called and left a message demanding answers. He was called back at 6:00 in the morning. When he inquired on why they were calling him at such an odd hour he was told: "That's how we roll". Then an HR employee scheduled a phone appointment to contact me regarding this issue. He did not call at the appointed time. When I called him 20 minutes after he was supposed to call, he said he was busy with other matters and rescheduled. He didn't call me back but called my tax agent at 7:00 a.m. in the morning and when my tax agent asked about my meeting being re-scheduled, he called me a liar. My tax agent was upset about this and brought this matter to the attention of his supervisor.

I subsequently submitted complaints to the Equal Employment Opportunity Commission (EEOC) and the Department of Fair Employment and Housing (DFEH).

I had applied for disability retirement as I was required to do for the LTD benefits. The Company does not pay into social security and had its own retirement plan. The Disability retirement medical examinations took years to complete. First, they sent me to an occupational medicine expert of their choice. He reviewed the medical records they sent him which at the time included about TEN medical reports indicating I was totally disabled with a work related illness. (Later on I had about TWENTY reports). Those TEN reports included the three Worker's Comp medical examiners including an internal medicine doctor, a psychiatrist and a neurologist. The occupational medicine doctor did all of his own testing and came to his own conclusions. He concurred with some of the doctors that I had Asthma/COPD and that I was totally disabled with a work related illness.

So I thought this would be a done deal. The disability retirement office would get the report and grant me the work related disability retirement. But it wouldn't be that easy at all. Next, they sent me to a Pulmonologist. The notice of the appointment they sent to me was dated 2 days AFTER the appointment. Fortunately, my attorney had confirmed the appointment with me and I was there on the right day at the right time. It became quite common for the medical appointment notices to have an error in either the date, time or location. I was baffled about why I was sent to a pulmonologist. I expected to be sent to possibly an ENT, infections disease specialist, internal medicine, etc. but a PULMONOLOGIST?

I was told the disability retirement agency has sole authority over which doctors I went to and which medical records they received. So I went to the pulmonologist and sat in the room and talked to him for a few minutes and the appointment was over. He wrote a report that said he needed to do his own testing. Months and months later I got a notice of an appointment for testing. I was not feeling well. I coughed every time I exhaled. The rattling noise from within my lungs could be heard audibly without a stethoscope. The pulmonary technician was concerned about my condition and called the doctor who told him to proceed anyway. I could hardly exhale into the machine at all without coughing. A simple check with a stethoscope would have confirmed the diagnosis of my regular doctor who two days later diagnosed me with Broncho-pneumonia. The pulmonologist concluded in his report that I was malingering.

Next, I was sent to a psychiatrist. My friend drove me and dropped me off. I was taken into the Doctor's office. The doctor's desk was at the front of a long narrow room facing down the length of the room to the back. I was directed to sit in a very low chair in the middle of the room so that I was looking up at him looming at me over his large high desk from far away. At lunch time I went to a small café about a block away, the only thing that was close. I saw him going for a walk past my outdoor table that was right next to the sidewalk and he just seemed odd. After lunch I completed the rest of the examination.

His subsequent report states "The applicant is incapable of performing all of the duties described in her class specification, and that she would have to work from home… That "if an employee cannot substantially perform the usual duties of the job and the condition is permanent in terms of recovery, that employee is incapacitated under Retirement Law." "The employee is permanently incapacitated in performing her usual duties…" "Thus, the exposure to Aspergillus, an industrial event, appeared to play a role… in having caused the employee's substantial impairment." My attorney explained the latin legal term to me: "Take the patient as they are." Regardless of pre-existing conditions, if the condition of the building caused any amount of my illness, then the cause is with the building. Although his report appeared to support my position, he was a very odd demeaning person.

Only later on did I do an internet search of the psychiatrist they sent me to and found the following comments:

> He was involved in a number of lawsuits both as Plaintiff
> & Defendant

In one of the Lawsuits, two women filed a petition for a protective order

I summarized the 36 online complaints against him below:

15 Complainants said he should not have the title "Doctor" / not be allowed to practice / should have medical license revoked / made complaint to medical Board / highly unethical

9 Complainants described a horrible experience, horrible man, the Patient was scared of him, he was a terrifying, horrific man.

9 Patients commented he needs therapy himself, should be a patient himself, Narcissistic, should be in solitary confinement with a mirror, he needs help for his own mental problems, sick man, unbalanced, needs help, staff is aware, looks crazy and could use help himself

23 complaints alleged: He was rude, had unprofessional behavior, inappropriate, out of line, patient disliked him, bad manners, strange man, worst doctor they ever met, emotionally abusive, idiot, poor bedside manner.

16 Patients complained: he caused their health conditions to worsen, they felt worse, he created more injury and harm

4 Patients complained of being kicked out of the office, dropped as a patient, yelled at and told never to come back, screamed at and told he never wanted to see them again, couldn't wait for patient to leave, didn't want to help anyone

18 Complaints indicated he was a bully, condescending, accused patient of being hostile, yelled at and belittled patient, erratic and berating behavior, emotionally abused patient

10 Patients said he was unfamiliar with their medication / prescribed meds conflicted with other meds/ meds had bad side effects / improper prescribing of controlled substances, he accused patient of not being compliant with meds, criticized, dismissed the opinions of other doctors

6 Patients complained his reports were biased, made up, lies, leading questions, did not wait for answers.

6 Patients indicated he only cared about the money said he was a money, grubbing freak and only cares about his pocket book, took advantage of people in need

4 Complaints about bias: He had religious bias, race bias, Complaints of him being mysogynistic, groped a patient, police were called, predator, intimidates women

10 Patients claimed he does not listen to/care about patient's mental health, he talked about his own life, was unfamiliar with patient's case, gave conflicting advice

8 Patients did not feel safe in this providers care, felt he was abusive to staff, people in office act as if they are fearful of him, doctor has a God complex, arrogant, feel he is dangerous, on a power trip

The reports from the psychiatrist and the pulmonologist were then sent to the original Occupational Medicine doctor and he was asked to reconsider his opinion (to reverse his original position that I was disabled with a work related illness). He said he stood by his original report and findings.

Then they sent me to their Ear Nose & Throat specialist. A review of the records he was provided showed he did not receive all of my pertinent medical records. He said he found no evidence of the Aspergillus infection and that I was not disabled.

Based on these reports, the retirement staff made a recommendation to their Board that my application for disability retirement be DENIED. My attorney then proceeded with an appeal.

In the mean time, my social security application for a finding of disability came up for a hearing before an Administrative Law Judge. It seemed that medical records were missing from my file. I made sure that all of the medical records got submitted. I found out that they were going to have an occupational expert testifying at my hearing. I immediately hired my own occupation expert to write a report. I provided him with my medical records and a summary of my condition and issues. He did his analysis and made a finding that I was unemployable due to my chronic illnesses, need for medical treatments and appointments (some weeks I ended up having seven and even eleven doctor appointments in a week).

I received the favorable report from my occupational expert and submitted a copy to the social security vocational expert. I thought that if he had already made an unfavorable report, it would be harder for him to back-track after he already testified. I wanted him to have the report before the hearing. Also, I had so many medical records, it was hard for anyone to look at them and understand the magnitude of my problem. Having this report to explain the situation would make it easier for him to come up with an accurate original opinion.

My brother drove me to the hearing. The judge explained there is a five step process: 1) am I involved in substantial gainful activity, 2) Is my impairment severe, 3) despite the impairments, what is my residual function capacity (RFC), 4) Evaluate my RFC and my past jobs and see if I could do any of those jobs, and 5) determine if there are any jobs in the work force that I would be capable of doing.

I answered questions about my work history and medical condition. The judge took the testimony of their occupational expert. At the end he asked him if I could do my past work and he said no. He was asked if there were any jobs that I could do. The expert said that I could do some kind of clerical jobs and gave the job code numbers and my heart sank. The judge looked at me and made a motion not to be dismayed. Then he asked the expert if I had to be off task more than 15% of the time, could I still do those jobs and His answer was NO!

It was months later when I received the official finding: Social Security found that I was disabled from performing any job in the national economy. I was very pleased that I had accomplished this myself without the assistance of an attorney. With that finding, I was now entitled to monthly monetary LTD Long Term Disability benefits from my employer. My last day of work was January 2012. It had taken several years of battles to receive the lump sum one year's worth of workers comp pay.

Now it was five years later. Worker's comp was not paying for any medical expenses which were substantial. The expenses averaged between $750 & $1,500 per month. I had been having to pay for the COBRA medical insurance and now the COBRA had run out. We had to convert to an individual medical policy that was much more expensive with higher co-pays and lower coverage. Now I was finally going to get a monthly LTD sum to be able to offset the medical expenses.

Now it was time for my Civil trial. The defendant's insurance company had transferred the case from a small law firm in San Diego to now be handled by a nationally renowned firm experienced in opposing mold cases. I had been advised that all previous offers were off the table. My Civil attorney was entirely un-prepared. I ended up having to make the enlarged exhibit boards and to make copies and put the exhibit binders together. There was a massive amount of exhibits that had to be copied, bates stamped and put in the exhibit binders. I knew his lone secretary was already overwhelmed and I pitched I and ensured that everything was prepared.

The first day of trial, two lawyers showed up on behalf or opposing counsel. There was a tall young good looking attorney and a shorter middle aged attorney obviously extremely experienced in public speaking and presenting cases. They had boxes of binders, exhibits and equipment. My attorney, when I hired him, was sixty years old with a booming courtroom voice and excellent memory of the details of the case, was now seventy with a croaking voice that was frequently inaudible.

It came time for jury selection and my attorney told me to signal him if I was unhappy with any of the proposed jurors. One of the juror candidates was a private investigator with a strong personality whose daytime job was investigations in opposition of workers comp cases. I did my best to signal my attorney I didn't want this guy on the jury but my attorney let him get on. I was shocked and felt that this guy alone could cause me to lose my case. Each day after the court proceedings, there were negotiations. After three days, they came back to the same offer made at the mediation. I was in a room with my attorney, the judge and opposing counsel and they all indicated I should accept the offer which I did.

The amount of the settlement is confidential. However, my elderly attorney decided not to pay me the money I was owed from the proceeds of the lawsuit and for a couple other matters he handled. I had to file a fee arbitration case with the State Bar. I filed and won the arbitration case by myself without an attorney but the attorney still refused to pay me. I filed complaints with the State Bar and he was disbarred. I hired a collection agency who had an attorney file for a judgment with Los Angeles Superior Court requesting a sum of money from him for all legal matters. There is also a client security fund the State Bar has to help clients like me. I'm still in the process of trying to collect either from the attorney or the fund.

In the mean time, my finding of disability at Social Security went to the department that determines how much disability pay you are to be issued. I already knew I was not eligible for any pay because of the special circumstance that my employer already pays into its own retirement fund. However, the Social Security staff that reviewed my claim, were not familiar with this situation and sent my file to the Appeals Council who proposed to reverse the Administrative Law Judge's decision because I was not entitled to disability pay and therefore should not have had a hearing. I was sent instructions on how to file an Appeal in Federal Court. I followed the instructions and submitted my appeal. I was very unwell and it was very stressful doing all the filings. I tried very hard to find an attorney and I quite by accident, ran across an attorney that specialized in federal appeals and knew how to obtain reimbursement from the government if we were to win. I was astonished that the opposing counsel, the federal government, would spend so much time and resources to keep me from getting.... NOTHING! My attorney came through and we won our federal case. The attorney filed the papers to be reimbursed for fees and expenses by the government at no cost to me. I was still eligible to collect my monthly LTD payments from my employer.

However, the original ruling of the Judge indicated the case should be reviewed in five years. Since the Federal Appeal took five years, it was now time for the five year evaluation. I had to obtain the last five years worth of medical records and go through a whole new process.

I still had bouts of very serious illness. Twice, I was so weak from throwing up, I passed out while I was vomiting. The first time I was kneeling in front of the toilet throwing up and when I regained consciousness, I was wedged between the toilet and the wall. The second time I was in bed and I was too weak to get up and throw up in the bath room. I scrunched up the comforter and threw up in it. I fell backwards I bed as I passed out. The soiled comforter was next to me on the bed for three days before I was well enough to get up and move it. I was unable to get up to eat during those three days.

When the office building I worked at was originally built, its 1999 base value of the property was assigned by the assessor at $4,657,436 according to the information still available on the government website. The 2021 taxable value approximately 20 years later was established at $6,745,581 by using a formula that increases the value of the property by approximately 2% per year.

The Governmental Board that oversees the agency I worked at, approved a 15 year lease of the property on March 2, 1999 to lease the building for $775,927 per year. In spite of the maintenance problems and in spite of the objections I submitted to the Board as part of the public comment process, a subsequent seven year lease was approved by the Board on April 30, 2019 for $6,682,200 over the seven year term or $954,600 per year.

So for the term of the two leases from April of 1999 to 2026, the government will have paid a grand total of $21,424,813 for a building that was $4,657,000 when built in 1999 and assessed at $6,745,581 in 2021.

In my objection letter to the Board, I explained and included all the details and attachments from OSHA's public file that indicated: 1) Chronic problems with the HVAC system, 2) Chronic & ongoing leaks, 3) Delays in repair work and repairs not done due to the owners non payment of invoices, 4) Air filters not changed timely, 5) No permit pulled for the $30,000 high pressure boiler installed on the roof, 6) Illness and pest complaints and failure to remedy them, 7) Past, ongoing and future liabilities to the company. I had the appropriate number of copies of my objection letter with attachments personally messengered to the Board in ample time before the deadline.

The leases were with the property owner, an LLC and the designated responsible signing person, whose names were also on the e-mails, work orders and checks, etc., in the OSHA file. A search of the public campaign donation website shows that the responsible signing person for this office building donated $4,600 to elections between 2007 to 2016 for the government officials responsible for the building and the approval of the leases. An affiliate LLP with the same responsible signing person donated $4,500 between 2010 & 2014 for the Board Members and elected officials responsible for approving the leases. The one official was elected and later arrested for reducing property taxes in exchange for campaign contributions.

So to summarize, the building owner donated at least $9,000 to the Board members that approved his leases that totaled $21,424,813 on a building that was valued at 4,657,436 when it was first built 21 years ago in 1999 and is now taxed at a value of $6,745,581. What a deal. And in spite of all the money paid on the leases, the building maintenance was in a state of disrepair with non-functional heating and air conditioning that made for a miserable and unhealthy work environment.

By late 2019, I had been feeling better but I had gained a fair amount of weight. My family and I talked about what kind of exercise program I could do. I did not want to go to a gym because I could get nose bleeds from the poor indoor air. Playing basketball again was absolutely out of the question as my lung capacity was now entirely insufficient for even regular breathing along with the risk of injury. I had arthritic knees, torn meniscus and torn rotator cuff in my left shoulder. I had doctor's orders for fresh air and sunshine and my right arm was one of the few body parts that was uninjured. So my daughter found a guy who gives tennis lessons. He would hit the ball in my strike zone and I could swing my racket in my right arm and hit it back. I enjoyed this therapy and I went a whole year without antibiotics and although I still had to use anti-fungal nasal spray daily, I felt I was on the road to recovery.

Thirty years ago, I made a wish list of all the things I'd like to do or have happen in my life. I recently came across my list and as I looked back on it, I realized I had accomplished all but two of the items on my list. I had met and married a great guy who was 6'-6" (who was taller than me, 6'-3") who I am still married to, travelled to Hawaii and Brazil, obtained a net worth of over a million dollars (easy to do in California when you buy a house for $640,000 and it increases in value to $1.1 million) etc.

One thing I had wanted to do was go to India and see the Palm Leaf Readers. These were guys who read ancient palm leaves. The story goes that years ago, there were visionaries who would have visions of the lives of people who lived in the future. They documented what they saw by writing it down on Palm Leaves. These leaves were now stored and you could go and have them retrieve your leaf and read about your life and future. When you showed up, they would measure your shadow along with the date and time you arrived to locate your leaf. Upon using matching points to verify it was your leaf, they would proceed to give you your reading. The writing on the leaves would have predicted where you were in your life at the time you came for the reading as well as future events.

I had recently seen where they were able to provide this service on line via zoom. Is it possible that some visionary would have seen my insignificant life and wrote it on a Palm Leaf? I thought, "What the Heck, I'll do it!" They have a foreign speaking person who is able to read the language on the leaves and a translator who relays the message in English. All I needed to do was send a thumb print and a fee and I was ready to go. No personal information such as name, birthdate, etc. were necessary. After a few days I was told they had obtained a number of leaves that could possibly be mine and an appointment was scheduled for a Palm Leaf reading.

The first part of the reading is ensuring the correct Leaf is found. They start off, having only had been given my thumb print saying the first leaf I have is for someone named X, whose mothers name is Y and fathers name is Z who has a certain number of brothers and a certain number sisters and children and was born on a certain date, etc. If any of these do not match, they immediately go on to the next leaf and repeat the questions with the names and dates on the new leaf. After doing this for about 25 minutes, I was beginning to think there was not going to be a leaf for me but eventually, they found a leaf with all of the correct matching points. Then they would take a break and give you your reading.

The matching points (names, dates and places) that were written on my ancient Palm Leaf that matched my life exactly were:

> My exact birth date and year
> Both of my parent's names and whether they are still alive
> My husband's name
> The names and genders of my children and whether they are alive
> The number of brothers and sisters I have

The aspects of my life that had already happened were spot on: the death of my son (saying that it was a Karmic relationship with his wife), issues with my work, application for retirement, etc. were all correct. Having just been through six years of hell with this Aspergillus fungal infection and workers comp and legal nightmare, my leaf said that I was two years into a period of the influences of the aspects of a bad Saturn and that the bad Saturn influences would last seven years. Holy Crap! The last six years did not suck bad enough already?! The good news is I was given some prayers and mantras to minimize the bad Saturn effects. I did each prayer in order as directed.

I had a recording of the reading and I had and I listened to it again because of the thick Indian accent of the interpreter. He said that following my upcoming xxxxx, several things were recommended. I listened to it a number if times and I thought he said SURGERY..., an upcoming surgery? But that had to be a mistake, because one of my goals in life is to never have surgery ever again. But after listening to it many times, I couldn't make out what else he would have said.

It was two years after the reading that I was diagnosed with Cancer. It showed up in an MRI of my spine. My spinal cord was being compressed and I needed to have immediate surgery to remove the cancer and prevent me from being paralyzed. Following the surgery, my legs were kind of wonky so I had to go to rehab after surgery, use a walker and work on strengthening my legs until I could walk normally. So OK, it could get worse than just having Aspergillosis.

I was told that the location in the spine was a secondary location and that the cancer had originated elsewhere but they never could pinpoint an exact location. The genetic markers in the cancer indicated it was lung cancer even though I had never smoked and there was no visible cancer detected in my lungs. So I began undergoing treatment for lung cancer.

I had a Pet scan from my hips to the top of my head but they could not find any source of the cancer. I found it odd to be treated for a cancer they couldn't find so I visited a number of different oncologists. I was amazed that one of them was actually familiar with Aspergillosis. He had treated a man for cancer. The man's cancer went away, only for the man to become infected with Aspergillus and later died of Aspergillosis. He said the mycotoxins from fungus / mold can cause damage to the genes that can cause cancer and that some types of cancer are unstable and unable to reproduce correctly and that after time, they die off because the copies of the copies of the copies of the cells can't reproduce.

Another one of the doctors I went to specialized in oriental medicine and anti-cancer alternative strategies. He had some products that in conjunction with radiation and chemotherapy, could help inhibit the cancer cells from reproducing. I also went to an internationally renowned cancer center in another state. Many famous international celebrities, presidents and dignitaries have been there. I believe in their patented protocol based on the same philosophy of causing the cancer to be unable to reproduce and based on what I saw with my own eyes. There was a five year old girl whose mother had been bringing her into the office in a stroller because she couldn't walk. She had been getting the treatment for a couple weeks. The next day when I saw her, she began walking and that staff was in tears to see her walk. By the day after, she was active and cruising around the doctor's office the way any child would be. Another day I was there, I saw a rather healthy looking "Good Ole Boy" from Texas who now lived a short ways down the freeway. I asked him why he was there. He said he was there for his final Pet Scan that showed his cancer was gone. He previously had a large tumor in his large intestine in October and now, here in March, using this treatment, it was gone. The lobby was covered with photos such as the brain cancer survivor group and such as photos of adults who had cancer as children and had been given only months to live by main stream doctors.

I had a great spine surgeon whose protocol mandated that I follow the prescribed radiation and chemotherapy regimens. So I had radiation treatment on my spine to kill and residual cancer cells and chemotherapy for systemic treatment to kill cancer. My oncologist was OK with me taking supplements which I liberally interpreted to include taking the Chinese herbs. As of this writing I am in the middle of my cancer treatments. My cancer markers have plummeted from a high of 35,000 to 399 (normal is less than 35). So I am optimistic about being rid of the cancer.

I have not had an appetite with the chemo. I ended up losing about 50 pounds. The weight I had failed to get rid of even with great effort, was now gone after 6 months.

In obtaining the details of the matching points my palm leaf reading to include in this book, I re-read the transcription of my reading. It said I would have a loss of weight and that I could manage my medical issues and that I would have ongoing medical expenses and treatment. It mentioned bone problems and that I needed to do walking as exercise.

If I was a cat and had nine lives, I would only have about eight of them left. I have come close to death many times. I've been using the processes described in this book to call for divine intervention to support and assist my cancer treatment and hope for a positive outcome. I'm not sure where this journey will end but I'm OK with wherever and whenever it does.

ABOUT THE AUTHOR

The author is married with two children and two dogs. Her first and only marriage is to her husband Gerry since 1985. Gerry has owned and operated his own successful contracting business since 1987. Her daughter Danielle played club volleyball and graduated from UC Berkeley with a degree in Public Health and has a Master's degree from San Diego State. Her son Bobby graduated from Cal State Fullerton with a degree in finance and insurance.

The author played two Division 1 sports in college, basketball and cross country and graduated from a Big 12 University. She worked in government and public service for around 25 years in the design, construction and maintenance of public roads, landscaping and facilities. She is a licensed property tax appraiser, licensed landscape contractor and certified electrical designer. She won over 15 State and local awards of excellence for her work in local government. She served on several local agency governing Boards in various capacities as President, Director, Vice President and Secretary.

She always tells her husband, who was originally from Belgium, that they should be proud of themselves. He came to the United States with only a few hundred dollars, about the same amount as what the author had when she graduated college. They always say, "we started out with nothing and we still have most of it left."

Printed in the United States
by Baker & Taylor Publisher Services